Two Minutes

An harrowing hospital tale beyond belief

by

Paul Stephen Pringle

RB
Rossendale Books

Published by Rossendale Books

11 MowgrainView, Bacup,
Rossendale, Lancashire
OL13 8EJ
England

Published in paperback 2012

Category: Memoirs

Copyright © Paul S. Pringle 2012

ISBN: 978-1-906801-81-6

Illustrations Copyright © Paul S. Pringle 2012

All rights reserved. No part of this publication may be reproduced, stored in a retrieval system, or in any form or by any means, without the prior permission in writing of the publisher, nor be otherwise circulated in any form of binding or cover other than that in which it is published and without a similar condition including this condition being imposed on the subsequent purchaser.

Dedication

To my wife Pauline. Daughters Michala and Natalie, and my son-in-laws David and Michael. My in-laws Graham and Kathryn. Also my dear friends who supported me all those terrifying months in hospital. Also the rest of my dear family & friends

Acknowledgements

To Professor G.L.Carlson and all the medical staff at Salford Royal Hospital (Hope Hospital) for saving my life. Without them I wouldn't have been here to write this book.

CONTENTS

CHAPTER ONE: *How It All Came About* 1

CHAPTER TWO: *The Investigation & The Diagnosis* 3

CHAPTER THREE: *The Operation* 11

CHAPTER FOUR: *The Disaster* 22

CHAPTER FIVE: *TPN - and those Damn Line Infections* ... 35

CHAPTER SIX: *C. Diff* 44

CHAPTER SEVEN: *Line Infection No. 2* 50

CHAPTER EIGHT: *Intensive Care* 57

CHAPTER NINE: *Where there's Hope there's Salford Royal* 70

CHAPTER TEN: *B4 - My new home for the next few months* 75

CHAPTER ELEVEN: *Home at Last* 86

CHAPTER TWELVE: *Return to Hope* 107

CHAPTER THIRTEEN: *The Big Operation* 114

CHAPTER FOURTEEN: *Intensive Care Unit* 118

CHAPTER FIFTEEN: *High Dependency Unit* 122

CHAPTER SIXTEEN: *Back to Ward B2* 125

CHAPTER SEVENTEEN: *Back Home* 133

CHAPTER EIGHTEEN: *Life with a megostomy* 154

CHAPTER NINETEEN: *Hopefully the last operation* 162

CHAPTER TWENTY: *Home for good* 168

CHAPTER TWENTY ONE: *Photographs & Illustrations* ...175

CHAPTER ONE

How It All Came About

June the first 2005, the new owner had taken over my business, allowing me to retire.

I had made it to the ripe old age of 57, in the March of that year. I had always planned to retire at the age of 55 but it did not work out. Well what's a year or two between friends? It might seem to you to be a bit presumptuous wanting to retire at 55, but there is a reason. When I was 18 years old my father died at the age of 60, long before he died he told me that he was so looking forward to retiring at 65, as he had had a very hard life. So after he died I made plans in my own mind, that if I retired at 55 I would at least have a chance of a bit of a retirement. I nearly didn't make it to the age of 60, as you will find out about further on in the book.

Over the past couple of years before I had retired I had had a villa built in Greece, on the island of Kefalonia, it was planned to be ready for occupation in September 2005, and I had a few things to tie up in the summer months before going to take possession of the villa in September, as it happened the villa wasn't ready when we arrived there, but that's another story.

Eventually when everything was finished we planned to stay there for a few months at a time.

My wife Pauline and I thought it would be a good idea to go to the Doctors for a check up, to make sure everything was okay so to speak. All the tests came back and everything was fine, except for one small detail.

For quite a while I'd had a show of blood occasionally in the toilet from my bum; I put it down to haemorrhoids bleeding after having a heavy night on the red wine.

My doctor wasn't having any of that and made an appointment with our local hospital, for an investigation to find the cause.

After a few months of waiting I received an appointment for late October which I duly attended.

Never having been to hospital for anything like this before, I didn't have a clue what was going to happen, so you can imagine my surprise when I was told to take my pants off, and to lie on my side with my knees up to my chest, then the doctor started to poke about up my bum with certain types of implements. During the investigation he found a polyp, (a polyp is like a wart), and it was growing on the inside of the bowel wall. The doctor then took a small piece of the polyp which was sent away for a biopsy to see if it was diseased, I believe that this is common practice on tissue that has been removed.

All my family were very pensive waiting for the results, waiting and waiting, it seemed like an eternity.

My daughter Natalie's wedding was taking place on the 5th of November, and as the day grew closer still no word from the hospital. In fact it was November the 4th at about 4pm, and I was at the hotel where the wedding was being held, when I received a phone call from the hospital informing me that the polyp was benign. The news being good every one was happy, and with the weight off my shoulders I could enjoy the wedding with a clear conscience.

CHAPTER TWO

The Investigation & The Diagnosis

Early November a letter arrived from the hospital, it was for an appointment for me to have the offending polyp removed, and to have a colonoscopy at the same time.

If you have never been involved with hospitals like I had not, or even if you have, some of the words they use don't mean a thing unless you have been to medical college. So I will try to explain them to the best of my ability.

A colonoscopy is basically an inspection of your large bowel and the distal part of the small bowel with a CCD camera, or a fibre optic camera on a flexible tube. This is inserted through your anus and pushed up the inside of the bowel to the colon, inspecting the bowl wall to see if there is anything there that shouldn't be there.

This procedure was arranged for early December, with the appointment came a parcel, containing 2 bottles of fleet, and the instructions when to take it, and how close to be to the toilet when taken. I have no idea how many readers have had a colonoscopy, or have taken fleet, but let me tell you, once you have swallowed that fluid it's like a steam train coming through, and if you are more than 5 yards away from the toilet, it's very likely you will need some clean pants.

The instructions were to take the fleet over 24 hours in stages before going to the hospital for the colonoscopy.

On arriving at the endoscope unit at the given time, I sat in the waiting area with a few other people all looking very pensive, and not really knowing where to look. After what seemed like forever, a nurse called out my name and took me into a room. She took my blood pressure, my pulse, my height, and my weight, then we filled out this form or should I say forms, it was like war and peace, talk about no stone unturned. I was then led to a cubicle to get changed into some light clothing, which I had been told to bring with me. I then sat in a draughty corridor with a few other people, waiting until it was my turn to go into the operating room. After I had been called into the room, I had to get on the table and lie on my left side with my pants pulled down, and my knees tucked up to my chest again. I was slightly sedated this time so it wasn't too unpleasant. When you are lying on the table, facing you is a large television screen, so when the camera is inserted in your bowel, you can watch the inspection, if you so desire. Before the camera was inserted, a large dollop of gel was introduced to help the camera slide more easily; I do believe that on the end where the camera lens is, a jet of air is blown out to slightly inflate the bowel, so that any infected area can be spotted.

It was quite interesting really looking inside your own body. After the doctor had finished the inspection it was time to remove the offending polyp.

Quite a clever bit of equipment this, because out of the end where the camera lens was, appeared a thin wire noose, which was manoeuvred round the polyp. When the noose retracted it cut the polyp off the bowel wall, and then out of the end where the noose had come from, came a three pronged pick up tool. It was like a claw which he picked up the polyp and retrieved it. As the polyp that I was the proud owner of was rather large, the doctor only managed to remove about 2/3rds of it. The doctor told me that I would have to come back in a couple of months to have the rest of it removed.

After I had been in the recovery room for a while, a nurse came to see if I was okay, and asked if I would I like to go to the toilet. She said don't worry if you are bleeding as it is a normal occurrence. So off I went to the toilet, (wow) I thought I had broke the pot, talk about a blast, it must have been all that air they had pumped up during the operation.

After my toilet episode they gave me a cup of tea and a biscuit then sent me home.

A few weeks later I received an appointment for the 22nd of December, to have the rest of the polyp removed, the news wasn't so good, as they had found some abnormality in the piece they had removed before.

I had been sent for quite quickly as they wanted to send the rest of the polyp away to be tested, it appeared they were quite concerned about the results of the last bit.

So I arrived at the endoscope unit as before, sat in the waiting area with all the other patients, everybody was still looking very pensive.

I don't know if you know it or not, but at the endoscope unit they don't only just insert the camera up the rear end, but also it is put down your throat. I have not had the pleasure of this procedure (yet), but it made me wonder if they use the same camera for both jobs. It crossed my mind; if they do I hope they wash it well. This reminds me of an old joke.

An army medical ward and the medical officer arrives on his rounds.
First bed M O says, rank name and number.
Patient says, Private Smith 98765 sir.
M O says what's wrong with you private.
Patient says bad case of haemorrhoids sir.
M O says treatment, good rub with the wire brush three times a day.
Patient says thank you sir.
M O says your ambition private.
Patient says to get back into the army as fast as possible sir.
M O says good man.
Second bed, M O says rank name and number.
Patient says, Private Jones 98147 sir.
M O says what's wrong with you private.
Patient says bad case of haemorrhoids sir.
M O says treatment, good rub with the wire brush three times a day.
Patient says thank you sir.
M O says your ambition private.
Patient says to get back into the army as fast as possible sir.
M O says good man.
Third bed, M O says rank name and number.
Patient says Private Wilson 87391 sir.
M O says what's wrong with you private.
Patient says tonsillitis sir.
M O says treatment, good rub with the wire brush three times a day.
Patient says thank you sir.
M O says your ambition private.
Patient says to be first in line for the wire brush sir.

Back to the endoscope unit and as before a nurse came and took me into a room, she took my blood pressure, height, etc, and another episode of war and peace. Next I went to the cubicle to get changed, but this time no draughty corridor, I had a surprise in store, I was taken to a little room with a bed and a toilet, the nurse then asked me if I'd had an enema before, I said no and she nearly broke into a laugh. I was told to pull my pants down, and lie on my side on the bed, pull my knees up to my chest. Does this sound familiar?

Well I have no idea how many readers have had an enema, but if you have you will know the score, but if you haven't, believe me its certainly different.

A large syringe is pushed up your bottom, the contents are then squirted in, you are then told to try and hold it in for as long as possible, I was told 30 minutes if I could; I managed to hold it for 20 minutes, then had to get to the toilet as fast as possible. This reminded me of my association with the fleet that I had taken a few weeks before. About 30 minutes had passed when the nurse returned, of course I was sat on the toilet when she came in, she enquired if I was okay, and said she would return in 15 minutes. The next time she came into the room I must have been suitably emptied out, because I was taken to the operation room, here we go again, lie on your side, knees up, camera inserted, and away we go. I'm getting so used to this routine now, I get into position without asking.

The person doing the operation this time was the main man so to speak, actually it was a woman. She was the consultant Ms Bronder, she is of German descent, a very nice person really, especially with the patients, but I believe she could be very hard on the nurses. This was the first time I had spoken to her, I had sort of seen her when I had had my first inspection, but I was laid on my side facing the wall when she came into the room, I didn't know it yet, but I was going to see a lot of Ms Bronder over the next few months. So it's back to the operation. She located the polyp, got the noose round it, but the stubborn thing just would not come loose. After about four attempts, and two new nooses, she managed to get it loose. She then tried to collect it with the claw, but she couldn't pick it up, she seemed to be trying for ages then another nurse said she had an attachment called a net. The camera was extracted and the net fitted, so the net went in, it was a bit like a fish landing net but with a draw string, that got the little devil!

After the operation Ms Bronder had a word with me about this polyp, she said it was a bit like a plant, and the roots could grow through the bowel wall, so she had put the wheels in motion for me to have a CT scan, and told me I would be receiving an appointment shortly.

So home we go and try to enjoy Christmas as much as possible. Christmas and the New Year passed, and we were all waiting anxiously for the results. Alas there was no news until the second week in January, when I received an appointment for a CT scan, on the 20th of January 2006.

The C.T. scan is done on a scanning machine that X-rays your body; I believe this machine takes pictures in slices. It is sometimes compared to looking into a loaf of bread by cutting the loaf into thin slices. When the imaged slices are reassembled by computer software, the result is a detailed multidimensional view of the body's interior. This should identify any problems; in my case it was to inspect the outside of the bowel, to see if the roots of the polyp had gone through the bowel wall.

On the Thursday 12th of January I received a phone call from a nurse at the hospital, the news about the polyp was not good, she said that it was not Malignant, but neither was it Benign, but it had abnormal cells, which could be 60% cancerous. She said that Ms Bronder thought it would be a good idea to remove it by taking away the piece of bowel where it was situated, what a dilemma! The nurse said that she would come round to our house, and discuss it with me and explain everything about the procedure.

The nurse that came to see us was called Jane, she was the local stoma nurse, and she brought some booklets and leaflets all about the operation, she explained the procedure, the fors and against. She said they could do the operation on Friday the 20th of January if I gave the go ahead, I told her about the C.T.scan that had been organised for that date, she said not to worry about that she would sort it, but I would have to have a C.T. scan before my operation.

After quite a bit of serious thought I decided I would have the operation as it seemed fairly straightforward, little did I know then. Before Jane left she told me she would ring me on Friday with all the details. Now our N.H.S. is called the Morecambe Bay Hospitals N.H.S. trust, and the Hospitals in the trust are, Furness General Hospital, at Barrow in Furness, Queen Victoria Hospital, in Morecambe, The Royal Lancaster Infirmary in Lancaster. The Ulverston, CHC, in Ulverston and the Westmorland General Hospital, in Kendal. So the schedule for the next week was hectic to say the least. Jane phoned on Friday morning, and said could I go to Westmoreland Hospital in

Kendal to see Ms Bronder at her clinic, to discuss my operation, and to make sure I still wanted to go ahead with the operation. Then go to Furness General over at Barrow in Furness for a CT scan on Wednesday the 18th, as the appointment I had for Friday at Lancaster couldn't be rearranged. Then to be admitted to Lancaster Infirmary on Thursday the 19th, ready for the operation on Friday the 20th. I myself live in Morecambe. What a whirlwind of a week; Barrow is about 45 miles, from home, Kendal is about 25 miles, and Lancaster is about 8miles, I didn't have much time to ponder about the operation that week, it was all go.

The meeting with Ms Bronder went OK, she told me about the percentages of the things that might go wrong, she explained all the procedure about the operation, this was to remove a section of the bowel which contained the offending polyp, and it wasn't certain whether I would end up with a stoma bag or not. She said it was a large operation and I would be in hospital about 10 to 14 days, and it would take up to 6 months to be back up to full speed. The odds seemed good, so I said I would go for it and signed the consent form. Little did I know then!

The CT scan at Barrow went OK nothing too scary about that.

On the Thursday off we go to Lancaster Infirmary to be admitted.

CHAPTER THREE

The Operation

I had been told to ring the hospital on Thursday morning about 8am to see if there was a bed available, of course you probably know the answer, it was no. I was told to ring back at 1pm. It was about 4pm when I actually arrived at medical ward 33 at the Lancaster Infirmary. I was allocated a bed, I was then given a blood test and a urine test, I had been told before going to the hospital not to have anything to eat on the day I was to be admitted, so you can imagine I was absolutely starving. Later that day a nurse arrived with a trolley with lots of things on it, she said don't get worried I am just going to put a *canula* in your arm, so I can connect this bag of saline to it to stop you dehydrating. For anyone who is not familiar with this procedure, a canula is a needle which inserted into a vein usually in your arm, it is attached to a square pad which is stuck to your arm, then the needle is removed and it leaves a thin plastic tube in your vein, on the end of the plastic tube is a little screw connector which connects to the giving set, which in turn connects to the bag of saline. Saline is basically water with a few additives which is held in place by a drip stand. (A drip stand is a long steel pole on a heavy metal base with wheels). On the top of the pole are arms to hook the bag on. The giving set is a long plastic tube which connects to the bag at one end and to the canula at the other end; it has an adjuster on it to regulate the speed of the fluid being given. I didn't have time to worry too much about my forthcoming operation, as for the first few hours was taken up by visits from doctors, nurses, anesthetises, asking all sorts of questions. Surprises, surprise, another portion of fleet just keep me busy for the rest of the evening.

Friday morning arrived and a nurse came with a tape measure, I thought it's a good job it's not a man in a black suit. With tape measure in hand she proceeded to measure my feet and legs for these bobby socks, these are long white socks with an hole in the sole, they are to stop deep vein thrombosis whilst in the operation, and during your recovery, the holes in the soles are a pain as they work round, and your toes pop through the hole, and become very uncomfortable, all fitted and ready, looking very sexy in my white socks!

I was taken to the operating theatre about lunchtime, before being taken into the theatre I was taken into the anaesthetic room which is at the entrance of the operating theatre. The day before, the anaesthetist came to discus the type of anaesthetic which would be best for this type of operation, and he made sure that I understood, and that I agreed with it. In the anaesthetic room an epidural was inserted, I had to sit on the side of the trolley and bend forward to curve my back, a local anaesthetic was injected into a small area of skin on my back, then a special epidural needle is pushed through the numb area and a thin plastic catheter is passed through the needle into your epidural space, the needle is then removed leaving only the catheter in your back, this is for the pain relief after surgery. I then had to lie on the trolley whilst they connected me to a blood pressure monitor; a breathing mask was placed over mouth and nose. I was told to count to ten, I think I got to two then it was good night Vienna! I can't remember a thing about the operation.

It was well into the next day when I arrived back in the land of the living, I was back on the ward and when I awoke, and after a quick inspection I was pleased to find that I hadn't been given a colostomy or in other words a stoma bag, which had been a possibility depending on the amount, and the position of the bowel to be removed. On further inspection in the area of the operation I found a long wound stitched with metal staples, it looked like a zip fastener. Whilst I was in the operating theatre and out of it so to speak, a catheter was inserted into my penis, so the waste could be transferred into a plastic bottle, which was fastened to the side of the bed. For the first few days everything seemed to be going fine, I had nothing to eat, and just a few sips of water, apparently this was to give the operation chance to heal. Ms Bronder came to see me on a regular basis, and on one of her visits she told me that the portion of bowel had been sent for biopsy, and the result was it was in the early stage of cancer, you cannot believe how relieved I was that it had been removed.

I received loads of get well cards, and a good share of visitors. I used to ring my wife Pauline in the mornings from the patient line, to let her know I was OK. The ward was quite large there must have been about 20 to 30 beds, so you can imagine it was very busy on that ward.

On the Tuesday morning I found that my stitches instead of healing had started to matter and weep. The doctor took a few of the staples out and said it could be my body reacting to the staples.

On Tuesday night I could not sleep and I didn't feel well, I asked the nurse if she could give me something to help me sleep, she said she didn't have the authority to give out drugs, she said she would ask the doctor but nothing came. I had to wait until the day shift came on and that was about 7.30 in the morning. So I rang Pauline and told her not to come on too soon as I had had a bad night, and I was going to try and get some sleep. It was about 3pm when Pauline and my daughter Michala came to see me. As they arrived on the ward they found the curtains pulled round my bed, there was a lot of activity as Ms Bronder with a few other doctors and nurses were fussing round.

Ms Bronder told Pauline she was very glad that she was here as she had some bad news. Ms Bronder took Pauline away from the bed and told her she was waiting for a theatre, as she had to do another operation because she thought that the bowel had burst, either at where it had been joined, or that some blood vessels had died due to handling. Pauline was very concerned but Ms Bronder assured her things would be okay, Ms Bronder told Pauline she was supposed to be going on holiday but she would put it off until she got me on the road to recovery.

Michala stayed with me at this time but to be fair I didn't have a clue she was there, I was fading fast. Later I found out I had got peritonitis, so some time during Wednesday afternoon I was rushed in to the operating theatre.

After the operation I was taken to intensive care and was there for 2 days, I don't remember much about my first time in intensive care, I think I must have been asleep all the time. You can't believe the strange effect that the drugs have on you, I had given a nurse a right telling off for not letting Pauline come to visit me, but she had been sat beside me at my bed nearly all the time I had been unconscious. I had to apologise to the nurse. Another thing, it must have been the drugs that gave you illusions, I felt like I was going up and down in a lift that never stopped for you to get out, (strange).

Back from intensive care to a new ward, medical ward 34. This ward was quite large, there were 2 bays with 8 beds each and 4 single rooms, 2 with toilets, and then there was a large bay for the ladies which had about 18 beds. So you can imagine it was a very busy, it certainly kept the nurses on their toes. I was taken to a bed by the window in one of the bays, I had a nice view out of the window and all the guys on that bay seemed quite pleasant.

The theatre attendant that brought me back to the ward was called John. I had known John for about 30 years he used to stay with us when we had a hotel in Morecambe. At this time John was working for a contractor, on the new Power Station at Heysham that was being built at the time. When I told Pauline she said I must have been hallucinating with all the drugs they had given me, eventually she met him and she apologised to me.

John was a regular visitor to me he used to call to see me after he had finished his shift before he went home, at least once or twice a week.

Now let me explain the Title of the book, as you can imagine the nurses are kept very busy, and what we don't realise how many nurses there are to look after so many demanding patients, so when you need a nurse you shout nurse, or push the nurse call button, when the nurse appears the reply is usually 2 minutes, after about 30 minutes you shout again, and if you are lucky the nurse may come to see what you want. When you have told the nurse what you require you are told I will be back in 2 minutes, so this usually goes on for a few times until you get what you need. If any reader has been in Hospital you will know what I am talking about. The thing is in defence of the nurses, if 6 patients ask this same nurse for 6 different things they would have to be a memory man to remember everything. But when you are laid in bed unable to do any thing for yourself, these 2 to 30 minutes, seem to take for ever, especially if you soiled the bed or some thing of that nature. I wish I had a pound for every time a nurse had said 2 minutes. But I must admit the nurses on ward 34 were fantastic, and attended to all my needs as best they could under the circumstances.

Whilst I was on the mend I discovered I had a stoma bag, this was alien to me, so a stoma nurse came to explain its use, and its reason for being there.

After my operation I wasn't coping very well and I don't think things were going well, so I had to have a pipe inserted down my nose into my stomach to remove all the excess bile. At this time my mouth was so dry, so a nurse brought some lemon flavoured swabs on sticks. They were like little lollipops. I had to stick them in a glass of water, then rub them round my mouth, I had to use these things on and off for a long time to come.

I had only had this pipe down my nose for about a day when something went wrong. I remember it was late evening and it was a young nurse who had to take the old one out, and replace it with a new one. She was frightened to death fitting the new pipe, she said that she had only fitted one before and had made a right pig's ear of it. It must have been my lucky day because it went straight down without a problem.

Another little problem occurred after a day or so. I say a little problem but what I should say is a very painful and quite a large problem. I contracted a water infection, and my testicles swelled to the size of small water melons. I was in terrible pain with them, so one of the nurses said they had a thing called a ball bag, which was supposed to take the weight and relieve the pain. She went to get one, she came back with the largest one she could find, but to no avail it was too small. Another nurse said they had some cream that would do the job. The nurse that came with the magic cream was called Hazel, she was what you might call a well built girl, and when she gave you a bed bath, boy you knew you'd had one, I think she was just a bit heavy handed, so you can imagine my concern when she arrived with the cream, but anyway she was quite gentle when she applied it, and it did seem to relieve the pain slightly.

I was told the infection had been caused by the catheter getting blocked. They then proceeded to remove the old catheter and replace it with a new one, and as you can imagine the procedure wasn't very pleasant.

During that day Pauline brought my grandchildren in to see me, Joe was only 4 years old and Maddie who was just 2 years old. Joe was frightened by seeing me with all the pipes and monitors which were connected to me in one place or another. I think he was so frightened he turned away and wouldn't look at me, it upset me a bit.

It was quite funny really because when they brought him at other times, he used to walk in sideways so he didn't have to look at me. On the other hand Maddie didn't seem to mind I think she was probably too young to understand what was going on. The only problem with Maddie was you had to watch her like a hawk so she didn't pull any of the pipes out.

After a day or so whilst I was on that ward I just seemed to start to go down hill, I was supposed to be getting better but to be fair I was just getting worse. I wasn't eating and a doctor called Mr Abraham came to see me, he was quite concerned and said he thought I should be connected to TPN; this is a food that is fed intravenously. It was the weekend and I had quite a few visitors, but to be fair I felt so ill I couldn't be bothered or even remember who had been. Apparently Rusty, and Denise, came to visit. They are two of our very good friends from Yorkshire. They were so upset at my condition they thought that would be the last time they would see me alive, in fact Rusty was so upset when they got back home he went straight to the pub for a good drink.

Everything just seemed to be in a haze on that Sunday.

I had a terrible night on the Sunday night, and on the Monday the nurses on the ward were getting quite concerned. By Monday evening there was a very funny smell coming from my body somewhere. I was not feeling very well at all and asked one of the nurses for a sleeping pill, she said she would have to get authorisation from the doctor. The doctor arrived and said he thought I should go for an X ray, the sister thought that it would be better to send for Mr Clark. Mr Clark was Ms Bonder's registrar. He was the surgeon on call for any emergencies that evening, so no further ado he was called for. Mr Clark was a super fellow you could talk to him, and he would tell you exactly what you wanted to know, and explain what they were doing to you and why. Anyway back to the plot, he took one look at me and smelt that awful smell. He ripped off my stoma bag and stuck his finger in the hole and said we will have to get you into the operating theatre as soon as possible before you die; he gave me the consent form to sign. I vaguely remember it said on the form life or death.

They then sent for Pauline, and just as she arrived they had me on the trolley ready to take me to the operating theatre, she said to Mr Clark, surely he can't stand another major operation. He said if I don't operate that I would die. Even when so ill, I said "let's get this show on the road" leaving Pauline and our neighbour Meryl in a sobbing mess.

Apparently I had pelvic abscesses; I believe it was quite a long operation, so after the operation I ended up back in intensive care for another 5 days. This was 3 major operations I had had in 2 weeks. After I had been in the intensive care unit for a couple of days I came round so to speak, I learned that the guy in the next bed was also very ill. I don't remember too much whilst I was there but I do remember the group Queen being played very loud. I later found out he had head phones on, it must have nearly blown his brains out.

His name was Billy, and eventually we ended up on the same ward and became good friends, and kept quite close after leaving hospital. Sadly he has passed away now.

I told you earlier about the hallucinations from the drugs. Billy told me when we were on the ward about his hallucinations, on a few occasions he had started to fight with the doctors and nurses, as he was certain they wanted to cut him up to put him into the Chinese food.

I said earlier I didn't remember much in ICU, but on the last couple of days of being in there I had got my faculties back so to speak. The nurse that was looking after me was lovely, she was called Katie, she took super care of me, and also the night staff had been very attentive, and ever so pleasant.

On the last night in there Katie introduced me to a nurse I had not seen before, she said she would be looking after me for the night. I can't remember her name but she was very large if you know what I mean. I nicknamed her Godzilla. I don't think I have ever met any one so heavy handed in my life. She came and settled me down for the night, I was trying to get to sleep when she started cutting cardboard boxes up quite close to my bed, she seemed to doing them for ages, then when she had finished she came to harass me. She wasn't happy with my urine output she said it must be blocking up, (yes you've got it), let's put a new catheter in just what you want in the middle of the night, especially with some one with such a gentle touch (ouch). Just getting to sleep and she's here again checking round and decides I could do with a new canular in the vein in my arm (ouch), I thought will Godzilla ever leave me alone. Eventually I got some sleep, 6 am she's here again saying I have to get you washed and ready for the day shift before I finish at 7.30 am, so a bit more torture what you might call a very rough bed bath will this nightmare never end ?

When Katie started her shift I told her about Godzilla, she said that she is usually very good; I most probably got her on a bad day or should I say a bad night.

Good news I should be going back to the ward today, so I was waiting patiently and trying not to take much notice of what was going on, as you can imagine a ward full of very sick people all connected to alarms it's quite unnerving. While I was laid there minding my own business, Dr Granger was doing his rounds with about 6 student doctors. He was explaining the problems that each patient had and he was asking the students individually how they would treat the symptoms. Eventually he arrived at my bed and the first thing he said was, here we have Superman and proceeded to tell them about my 3 major operations in 2 weeks, and how well I had recovered and about all the problems I had encountered over the last 2 weeks.

I had been waiting all day to be taken back to the ward, I kept asking Katie why I had to wait so long, she said they were waiting for a bed, I was beginning to think I might not get on to the ward today, and have to suffer the wrath of Godzilla again. But unbeknown to me they were waiting for a vacant operating theatre, to put some gauze over the great big hole in my tummy. Apparently there had been a room on the ward from about 1pm, and as I found out later Pauline and Michala had been waiting for me to be brought back from intensive care. As Pauline is a stickler for everything being super clean and to kill the time they had given the room a right good clean.

It was about 4pm when Ms Bronder came to see me, she said I would be going to the ward in about 30 minutes via the operating theatre, (not there again), I had never been to the theatre as much in my life, I don't recommend the presentation though.

Eventually I was taken back to ward 34, I was given a side room but little did I know then it was going to be my home for the next 5 months.

CHAPTER FOUR

The Disaster

The room on the ward they gave me was quite nice, there was a lovely view over the car park looking across to Lancaster Castle, and the Lake District was in the background. I forgot to mention it before, but when I was on this ward previously also, if you remember, I had a bed next to the window in this ward. Whilst I was on this ward they had started to build a massive new pharmacy in the car park; at the time I was there they started to erect the steel stanchions. In my new room I also had a view of the new construction, so it was a bit of interest to me to watch the building work going on as I recovered.

The next day when I felt more with it so to speak, I had an inspection to see what they had done to me, I found I still had a stoma bag but now it was in a different place, I had a plastic tube coming out of each side of my waist, to drain off all the excess fluids away. I still had my catheter in (the one that Godzilla kindly tortured me when fitting it).

I had a great big dressing over my tummy, a canular in each arm and an oxygen mask over my mouth and nose.

Now this hole in my tummy was very large and it needed constant attention, so the nurses came quite regularly to change the dressing. It was a constant mess all these fluids running out of the bottom of the dressing down between my legs. It was quite hard to seal as the wound was low down on my tummy, the size of the hole was about 9 inch, or 23cm, by 8 inch, or 20cm, and 2 inch, or 5cm deep.

Ms Bronder and Mr Clark used to come and see me every day to check on my condition. Mr Clark tried a few times to make the dressing stop leaking all over the place, he brought some fancy yellow tape that was supposed to be the best thing since sliced bread, but that didn't work either.

This was about the time they thought that a vacuum assisted closure system might be the best thing to use; these machines are called VACS for short.

These machines are hired in by the NHS, so a specialist nurse from the company had to come and inspect the wound, to see if the VACS machine was suitable for this application. When she came I don't know if she was in a hurry or not, but she only lifted the top bit of the dressing and said it would be okay. Now I would have thought you would have to take all the dressing off to see if it was suitable, but I am only the patient, and she was supposed to be the expert.

It took a few days for this machine to arrive, probably a lot of forms to fill in, and some one had to give permission for the machine to be hired.

Eventually it arrived and a nurse called Brenda got the job to fit this thing, apparently she had been on a course to fit these machines. I will explain this machine to you, it's a piece of foam rubber about 2 inch, or 5cm thick that is cut slightly smaller than the size of the wound, and placed in the hole, then an adhesive sheet like cling film, is placed over the top and stuck to the surrounding area, then a small hole is made in the centre of the adhesive sheet, then a small connector is fixed into the hole. It is then connected with a plastic tube to a machine that sucks all the excess fluids into a plastic collection pot, and supposed to close the wound.

Brenda was a very good and efficient nurse; she had been a nurse for more than twenty years. When she came to fit it she said that she was not happy fitting it on an open bowel wound, she said I have never fitted them on a wound like this before. They are usually fitted on amputations, or similar wounds. She said I am going to go and get a second opinion on this. She got in touch with Ms Bronder and she said it should be fine as she had put some gauze over the wound which covered the bowel. Brenda still wasn't happy so she contacted the firm that supplied the machine. They said to put about 5 sheets of gauze between the bowl and the foam and it should be okay. So it was fitted and switched on and everything seemed fine, it was a great relief to me as all the mess stopped running down my legs.

All of a sudden things seemed to be getting better; I was allowed to start eating, and with assistance I was got out of the bed and into a chair by the window, it was the first time for a week or two that I had seen the outside world.

On the wards and in the rooms each bed had a television set on a big long arm which was fastened to the wall, this allowed the television to be watched at any angle, and also be pushed back against the wall out of the way. This is called the patients line, it's quite expensive, but it is a god send when you are in hospital for a long time. It is not just a TV but a radio, a computer, a games consul and a telephone. You were allowed access to the patient line by the purchase of a card which was inserted into the set.

It was handy having a telephone next to you in bed, as I used to ring Pauline on a regular basis, it was also good that Pauline could ring me direct and not have to bother anyone else.

Pauline was a tower of strength to me as she used to come to the hospital for 2pm, and stay until 8pm when visiting finished, which helped no end because if you were on your own the days seemed to last for ever.

Every day I was getting stronger but still needed help to get out of the bed into the chair, and I still had all this stuff attached to me, so I had to be careful not to catch anything that was dangling.

Now it was time for the physiotherapist to see if they could get me walking, up to now the physiotherapist had had me doing breathing exercises, and leg exercises laid in bed. So the two of them got me on my feet, one at each side, and gathered up all the equipment still connected to me, which consisted of a pipe out of each of my sides with a collection bag fixed to them, a catheter with urine bag, the vacs machine, a drip stand with a bag of saline on it. I think I managed about 6 steps then I went dizzy. I couldn't believe how weak I was.

A bad habit I had got into whilst laid in bed, or sat in the chair with my legs up, was to cross my legs, the physiotherapist kept telling me off for this, saying that it could cause blood clots after an operation,(by the way I still had to wear my sexy bobby socks). Another person that gave me stick about crossing my legs was Sue, she was one of the sisters on the ward, if she saw my legs crossed she used to flick my toe with her finger nail, and say naughty boy, she was really nice and was always very concerned about my condition.

Another thing about my bobby socks, if I was laid on the bed and my toe had happened to come out of the hole that was supposed to be on the bottom of the sock, and when Ms Bronder came into the room she would start to squeeze my toe, I am sure she must have a foot fetish, as every time my toe was visible she would squeeze away.

Well back to the vacs machine, and the foam needed to be changed every 36 hours, all the nurses commented on how well it seemed to doing.

My health kept improving and my stoma seemed to be working well. I started to get more visitors, and I can say I was really pleased to see them all, many friends and family from far and wide. In my own mind I thought things were looking up.

It was very nice in my little room, but there were good things and there were bad things about being on your own, some times you missed the company of the other patients on the ward, and when you needed a nurse, trying to catch them as they passed the door. If I couldn't I would push the nurse call button, but some nurses didn't like you pushing the button unless it was an emergency, anyway when eventually you did get a nurse the answer usually was 2 minutes.

The regular nurse visits were to take your observations, which were your blood pressure; you're breathing, your pulse, and your temperature, to get you out of bed, washed and dressed for the day, to change your bed, and with the meals at meal times.

As I mention meals, I was starting to eat quite well now, and my stoma seemed to be working correctly, there was talk of me going home soon. I had been in hospital about 1 month now so going home sounded good to me.

The good thing about having you own room was, being nice and quiet especially at night, and be able to watch television undisturbed, it was also private when people came to visit, I think that probably the nicest thing was, I had my own wash room, and not having to share with others.

On the Wednesday 22nd of February I was told if they could organize a machine for home, it was likely I could go home on Friday. I thought fantastic I will be home for my birthday. The machine you have at home are a lot smaller than the one you have in hospital, so someone from the company that rents the machine's had to come to my house to make sure I new how to work it.

Well Friday arrived and I was waiting pensively to go home, when we received a message, that the lady, who was going to bring the machine to my house, could not come today, it had turned out that her little girl had an accident, so it would be Monday now before I would be able to go home. Never mind what's another day or two when you are going to get home.

I think it was on the Thursday morning that the vac pac was changed, and the nurse that changed it was not a regular nurse on this ward. I don't know whether she was familiar with this procedure but she only put one piece of gauze between the foam and the wound. It still makes me wonder if this had anything to do with my next problem.

During the Friday afternoon I was a little concerned about how quickly the collection pot on the machine was filling up, so I told a nurse but she didn't seem too concerned, as it happened the foam needed to be changed on Friday evening. On the Friday evening the nurse arrived and took the piece of foam off the wound, to mine and her surprise these lumps had appeared up through the gauze, so a doctor was called he said we had better contact Ms Bronder. She was contacted but was not able to get to the hospital that evening, she told them to put a dry dressing over the wound, and dispense with the vacs machine, and she would see me in the morning.

Well that just put pay to me going home for a while.

Saturday morning and Ms Bronder arrived; she had the nurse remove the dressing, and a look of amazement came over her face, she said, oh dear it look's like foetus, and proceeded to cut through the gauze, which caused the foetus to spout out like a fountain, this was the start of a very messy week to follow.

What had happened was, that the small bowl, (on which the vacs machine had been on), had formed 5 holes, the technical term is fistulas. Now I truly believe that it was the vacs machine that sucked these holes in the bowel.

At this time I didn't know the problems that this would cause, I thought they would just take me back to the operating theatre and fix it, but apparently it doesn't work like that.

Unbeknown to me at this time, this was a very serious problem; anything to do with a perforated bowel could take a very long time to sort out.

The first thing that Ms Bronder did was to push some rubber tubes down these holes, and connect them to some collection pots, that was a waste of time the foetus just came up on the outside of the tubes.

Now I had just got used to eating again and once again that pleasure was to be taken away from me, because everything that went down your throat came out of these fistulas.

The next problem was trying to mop all this mess up which was coming out of the wound, and out of these fistulas. Now you can imagine that there are a lot of patients to get up washed and fed in the morning, and only a few nurses to see to this task. Well I must say I felt a little neglected sometimes in my little room, and it wasn't very comfortable laying wet through, and this green bile coming out of these fistulas, which burned your skin. I started to get very down trying to get a nurse to come and clean me up in the mornings, and when getting the attention of a nurse only to hear, I will be back in two minutes.

So I asked the sister if Pauline could come to the hospital early in the mornings to clean me up, I know you shouldn't have to do this, but if you had seen the state of me in the mornings, I was in absolute agony with this bile.

Now they have things called wound management bags for such wounds as mine, but the problem was they didn't have any large enough to cover this large hole in my tummy. Now not eating or drinking again another canular had to be fitted, and I was connected back to the intravenous food (TPN). It is actually called, Total Parental Nutrition, and it is actually prepared for each individual patient. They take a blood sample before the food is prepared, so if you have any deficiencies it can be added to the food.

I think it was about Thursday when they eventually found a wound management bag large enough to do the job. The fitting of the bag was down to the stoma nurses, the only problem here was, they only worked Monday to Friday, and I needed a new bag every day. Changing the bag was no mean task it took about 60 to 90 minutes to put a new one on, and as there were only a couple of stoma nurses for our area who were supposed to fit the said bag, but that didn't always fit in with there schedule. The nurses on the ward also used to put them on, but they really didn't have a lot of time as they were so time consuming, so Pauline to the rescue again, she learned how to fit them.

The bags that they had found me weren't really up to the job, so the stoma nurses had to keep trying different companies until they eventually they found one that would do the job. I will explain these bags to you, the size of them was 12inch, or 30cm, by16inch, or 40cm, the front of the bag was clear plastic with a round window that opened, it was about 5inch, or 13cm, in diameter, it had a spout with a plug at the bottom, and a self adhesive back in which you cut an hole the size of your wound.

This bag is stuck to your body around the wound, and catches all the fluid that comes out of the wound, and out of the fistulas. This dark green bile I mentioned earlier is created in your stomach to break down the food when it gets there; apparently the body makes about a litre of this stuff a day, and take it from me when it gets on your skin it burns like mad. It is very to hard to keep the bag on your body for any length of time, as this stuff eats through the adhesive. The problem with getting the adhesive on the bag to seal was that the area around the wound had to be as dry as snuff, and the most annoying thing was sometimes everything was ready, that bile stuff would spout out, I had no control over this part of my body, and it would release at the most inconvenient times.

Mr Clark told me one day that this bile stuff was so potent, that if you poured some on to a piece of steak, it would eat through it in no time.

They were at a bit of a loss with me and my fistulas, as it had been 3 years since they had had anyone with a fistula at Lancaster. Ms Bronder said she would contact Salford Royal Hospital Manchester, also known as Hope Hospital, as they have an intestile failure unit there, which deals with problems such as mine, so she could find out the best way to deal with my problem!

Ms Bronder and Mr Clark both felt sure that these fistulas would heal up, apparently the patient who had had the fistula 3 years ago; it had healed up, so I think they probably thought mine would do the same.

I had been in hospital for quite a while now, and I really hadn't had a good shower or a bath, no matter how good the bed baths were they were no substitute for a real bath.

So I asked if there were any chance of a proper bath, to my surprise I was told yes. This was a bit of a challenge, a lift was brought which looked a bit like an engine lift, then I was put into a sling and hooked on to this thing, my modesty was covered with a big towel and then I was pushed into the bathroom swinging about on this thing.

I was lowered into the bath and it was absolutely fabulous, it just felt so good to have a proper bath. This little adventure didn't come without its problems though, as I was lifted out of the bath my bag decided to come away at the bottom and all this gung ran down my legs, you can't win! All nice and clean and this happens.

At this time the dietician stepped in to help with finding me the nutrition I needed extra to the TPN, his name was Tim. I liked Tim, he was good to get along with and he kept me informed on what was going on, he was also in touch with the dietician at Hope hospital to make sure I was given the right nutrition.

I was being fed by TPN as I said before, but now I had to start to drink 2 sachets of dioralyte mixed in 200 ml of water 5 times a day. Dioralyte replaces body fluids and salts and it comes in 3 flavours, citrus, blackcurrant, and natural, this one you can mix with cordial to get different tastes, but of course at Lancaster they only kept blackcurrant flavour. So good old Pauline to the rescue, she used to call at the chemist on the way to the hospital, and buy some different flavours, blackcurrant was very nice, but 5 times a day every day, no thanks.

I also had to drink a build up food called forty sips, these were a very high protein drink, so this was my diet for the next few months, I did try a little to eat, but it just caused loads more stuff to come out of my fistulas, so I had to knock that on the head.

It was a constant job for Pauline fitting me with new bags, so I was pleased to be in my little room for the privacy, I say privacy that was a joke. The door to my room had a window in it, with a screen that could be opened and closed from either side, so that the doctors and nurses could look in on you to see if you were okay without disturbing you. Now you will not believe it, but many times as Pauline was changing my bag, visitors would open the screen to look in, (nosy sods), so Pauline would try to wedge it closed before she started.

As the days past by I got stronger and eventually got rid of my catheter, I say got rid of my catheter, gosh it could only happen to me!

When these things are fitted in place, you have no feeling of passing water, or of wanting to go to the toilet.

Well my good friend Pete, who lives in Manchester came to visit me, he was on his own that day, as is wife Sue who was suffering from cancer, had a chest infection and didn't want give it to me. Anyway Pete, who is well known for being a bit clumsy, on leaving my room he tripped over something, it wasn't until later that we found out what he had tripped over. Pauline was about to go for her tea and I said to her I had a funny feeling, like I wanted to go to the toilet, she said that's strange you have never felt like that before have you, I said no and off she went for her tea. After a little while it was getting quite painful, so I called for a nurse, she said my catheter had been dislodged, so she took it out for me.

When Pauline came back I told her, she said Pete must have tripped over the catheter bag and dislodged it, well never mind it was one less thing to worry about.

Another little problem were these bed sores that had appeared on my bum, apparently these had been caused by being in bed, and by being helped slide up the bed to sit up. I think it must be the friction of your bum sliding up the sheet that breaks the skin. Now for some reason it never seemed to heal, this was a thorn in my side, or should I say in my bum, for a long time to come.

I was walking a lot better now with the help of the physiotherapists , and had started to be able to get out of bed to the chair on my own, I could watch the building project out of the window, and I was starting to get my interest back now, as before I just couldn't be bothered. Its funny but at certain times you think you are never going to get better, and as it was my first time in hospital I couldn't believe how it could knock the stuffing out of you so much.

    I was getting my fair share of visitors now, they boosted moral no end, and of course the impending birthday came and went, so much for being home for that event, anyway I received lots of cards and made the most of a bad job.

CHAPTER FIVE

TPN - and those Damn Line Infections

Now can I tell you about this TPN? The ones I had were a two litre bag of like a thick milky substance, which hangs on a drip stand. This is fed through a giving set, which goes through a machine, which regulates the amount of fluid that is fed into your body. At this time I was being fed through a canular in my arm into a vein. The problem with this is that the TPN is very strong, and after it has been flowing through your vein between 24, and 36 hours, it breaks the vein down, and the TPN would not pass through it. Consequently your arm around the canular would start to swell up, so a new canular had to be put in to another vein, so you can understand that after a while trying to find a good vein became a bit of a problem. It apparently takes a long time for the vein to repair itself.

For patients who are on long term TPN, they put a line into your chest into a major artery; this is called a main line or a Hickman line.

I bet you can't guess? Yes you are right, another trip to the operating theatre, this time just a local anaesthetic. As before I was taken to the anaesthetic room outside the theatre, and connected to all the usual things. In the theatre they put me on the operating table using a patient slide, or a pat slide this sounds very technical, but it's not really, it's just a piece of shiny plywood, that they slide you from one bed to another.

Well now they have got me settled on the bed a nurse shaved my chest, and then proceeded to paint my chest with this brown antiseptic fluid. Then covers were placed all around the area that was going to be worked on, they then put like a curtain across the front of my face so I couldn't see what they were doing. The table was then tilted back; I was then given the local anaesthetic, all ready to go now.

The doctor said if he hurt me I had to shout. First I felt a slight incision, then he slipped the tube in, I didn't really feel that, but then he started push really hard on my chest, I thought he was going to break my ribs. Then he put a stitch or two in and that was me done, except for the x-ray to see if the tube had gone into the right place.

After the operation I was taken into the recovery room, I was there for about 2 hours, then before I left a nurse removed all the bits and pieces, I had another x-ray, then I was taken back to my lovely little room.

Later that day the TPN was connected to the new line in my chest, it felt good not to have a line dangling out of my arm for a change.

After a day or so I started to walk about unaided, I did use the drip stand to support me, I couldn't go anywhere without it as my TPN was on there, and I was connected to it 24 hours a day. It was fantastic now that there was nobody having to come and try and fined a good vein to put a canular in every other day.

Now having to be connected to this TPN for 24 hours a day, you would think that there would be a bag available when it was needed? (No), I can't remember the amount of times that the TPN wasn't available when it was needed; this problem came about because a doctor had to sign a form or something, as the pharmacy would not send it to the ward without a doctor's signature. Now you would think when a patient's life depended on this stuff, and everybody concerned new about it, that a system would be in place that a bag would be ready to use when it was needed. The longest time I waited for a bag was 16 hours, and I can tell you I felt very weak by the time it arrived. I used to ask the nurse about my TPN when it hadn't arrived she would tell me it hadn't been signed for, so I would have to wait awhile. Another thing this TPN was supposed to be kept in the fridge on the ward until it was time to be connected, but in many cases it was just left out on the top of the desk, or a cupboard.

Now can you remember I mentioned Billy when I was on the intensive care unit? Well he was brought on to ward 34, and he was in the next room, so I thought I would go and visit him. When I got there he wasn't very well, I think he had been on the intensive care unit for about 5 weeks.

I didn't know at the time but Pauline had become friends with Billy's partner Lynn, they used to meet to have a meal together in the bistro at the hospital.

As Billy got better we became good friends, and later on in the year when we were much better, to relieve the monotony, we would walk round the hospital corridors. We looked a right pair, as Billy needed 2 walking sticks to enable him to walk, (I nicknamed him Billy 2 sticks) and I was pushing a drip stand. Many times doctors and nurses would stop us on the corridors, and ask us where we were going when we were at the other end of the hospital. We would tell them we were trying to escape, or going to the pub, just down the road.

It was well into March now and I was having lots of visitors, but one of the most regular was my best friend Derek and his wife Denise. They came from West Yorkshire to see me every Thursday evening without fail.

Derek is a bit of a card and always had a tale to tell, and was always trying to make me laugh. My operation hurt like mad when I laughed but I didn't mind. Another thing he would bring me sweets and chocolates which I couldn't eat, but I didn't mind watching them eat them.

I remember one time; Denise asked if she could have a look at my wound through the bag. When Denise was looking, Derek took a look and nearly fainted, he had to sit down and suck on a sweet for awhile to bring him round. Denise said it served him right he shouldn't be so nosy.

One time Derek said he couldn't believe what I had gone through, and if it had been him he would have thrown a rope around the TV arm and hung himself.

Pauline's sister Kate and her husband Graham also came once a week, their day was Sunday. They also came from Yorkshire, they could be classed as being a bit more serious than Derek, but I was still very pleased to see them every week.

There were always hospital personnel popping in, such as countess Dracula. This was the blood nurse she would arrive every third day, and relieve me of four tubes of blood. When she took the blood she would put a tourniquet on your arm and find a good vein, then as she was going to stick the needle in she would say (sharp scratch), this is something else I wish I had a pound for.

The pain nurse would call every other day to see if I had any different pain, or if I was coping with everything, she was a really nice lady.

And then there was Elaine, she was the cleaner, she was ever so chatty, and always seemed very concerned about my condition.

March seemed to pass without much problem, I wasn't getting much better, but on the other hand I wasn't getting any worse.

One day I was walking round the ward to the best of my ability, and one of the pipes in my side fell out. These were the ones to drain of the excess fluid, to be fair there was hardly anything coming out of this one now. Mr Clark said it would be okay, I had a funny feeling he might try and stick it back in, anyway, blow me but 3 days later the other one fell out. The difference was this one was still putting a fair amount of fluid out, a couple of days later I felt as if I wanted to go to the toilet, I thought that's strange, my bottom is supposed to be stapled up. I told Ms Bronder she said it was probably the pus that had been coming out of the pipe, and it was making its way down there, she said that was good, and I had to collect some when it came out of my bum, so it could sent away to be tested. It came out okay at the beginning, but after a while it stopped, I still had the feeling and it started to get quite painful.

Its no fun in hospital more torture, a junior doctor arrived with a large syringe and a bowl of water, she told me to lie on my side, knees up to my chest, (remember this position), this syringe had a tube attached to the end of it, which was inserted into my anus, then this pus was sucked out, some water was then pumped in then sucked out again, I had the pleasure of this procedure, twice a week for the next 6 or 7 weeks.

Amongst all this excitement I passed the time by reading quite a lot and being clerk of works watching the building work going on outside my window.

It felt now that every thing seemed to be going well, as I was feeling a lot better, and being able to walk around the hospital.

This was until one morning when I woke up and I felt absolutely awful. I couldn't lift my head off the pillow, I told the nurse and she went to get a doctor, he arrived and after a quick inspection he pronounced I had got a line infection.

It appears that this TPN that was being pumped into my main artery wasn't being looked after properly. Apparently when the bag is changed, the connector on the line has to be kept clinically clean; otherwise it is prone to infection.

I didn't know how critical this was, until later in the year when I managed to get to Hope hospital.

The first thing they did was to disconnect the TPN line and send for the microbiologist. This line infection made me feel like I were frozen, in actual fact I had a raging temperature, so all the bed clothes were pulled off me, and a fan placed next to my bed on full blast, and was given some paracetamol and I was then connected to a blood pressure monitor, as my blood pressure had gone sky high.

It was the microbiologist's job to find an antibiotic to get rid of the line infection; apparently each case is different so the same antibiotic can not be used on different patients.

What happens is the blood gets infected, and it causes like a fungus, which travels through the body at an alarming rate, and I couldn't believe how bad it made me feel, in such a short time.

So out come the canular's again, they had to put a canular back into my arm, to be able to put the antibiotic in to my body, but to be fair the microbiologist got the infection under control fairly quickly. I think I was taken to my bed for about a week, you know you begin to think why me.

Anyway back to the old problem of finding a good vein to put the canular in, apparently I had to wait a couple of weeks before they could put another line into my chest, they had to make sure all the infection had long gone. So I was a bit like a pin cushion again.

Another problem was that these fistulas were getting bigger, and nobody seemed to know what to do with them. Pauline and myself kept asking Ms Bronder if I could go to Hope hospital for a second opinion, or for a doctor to come from Hope to come and see me, it was to no avail, she said she was trying to get me onto the waiting list, to go as a patient to Hope, and be treated down there. Pauline and I felt we were just getting nowhere.

Well a few weeks passed, and I had another line put into my chest, in the other side this time, it had meant another trip to the operating theatre. But when I came back with a new line, I was asked, if I would mind if a Macmillan nurse could come and, show the nurses on the ward the correct way to connect the TPN. (Possibly to minimise the risk of line infections), apparently this same system is used for cancer patients when they are given chemotherapy, so I agreed, I thought if it means no more line infections, she can do what she likes.

Billy 2 sticks had also taken a turn for the worse, at about the same time as I had had my line infection.

Here we go back on my feet again, walking about the ward, and generally getting in the way trying to pass the time as best I could.

About this time Billy 2 sticks was getting a bit better and managing to get about a bit, he had to walk with a Zimmer frame now but that didn't hold him back much, and I was walking with the aid of my drip stand. Still we managed to have a walk on the corridors, the only trouble I had was this dam bag that was on my body. I would just get into the corridor, and I would feel something running down my legs, so I had to get back to my room and get myself padded up and lie on the bed until Pauline came and put a new bag on, this got on my nerves a bit as it was a regular occurrence.

I had started to lose quite a bit of weight now, actually it was over three stone, and as one of my visitors said, it was a bit of a drastic way to diet.

Then one day one of my visitors brought me a jigsaw puzzle, so one of the nurses found me a piece of hardboard from somewhere to put it on. Of course this caused a landslide of jigsaws; nearly everybody that came to see me brought a jigsaw.

I started doing these jigsaw puzzles and I will say they get quite addictive, and then to my amazement some of the nurses started to put pieces in, when they came into my room, I think they got addicted to it as well, in fact when a nurse came into my room, I thought they were coming to see me? No they put some more pieces in the puzzle.

I used to rest the board that I did my jigsaw on, on the window bottom, it was a bit unsteady but if you were careful it was okay. Well one day I nearly finished this puzzle I think it was about 1,000 pieces, when a new doctor came in and lent on my jigsaw board, what a mess there were jigsaw pieces all over the floor. After that episode when I had finished doing it for that day, one of the nurses would take it and put it on the top of the filing cabinets in the corridor outside my room. From my room when the door was open I could see the nurse's station, and the desks they used for doing there paper work.

I remember one evening and I think I must have been dozing, when I awoke I noticed the nurse's had taken my jigsaw puzzle on to their desk, and they were very engrossed adding pieces, I thought what a liberty.

Continuing, Billy and I started to venture a bit further round the hospital, bag permitting, and when we weren't walking, Billy would spend most of the time in my room. He was right good company, and we got on like a house on fire.

Now we had both been here for quite a while, the nurses said they were going to put our names down for the Christmas party.

I had been in this room that long now they had started to call my little room, Paul's room.

CHAPTER SIX

C. Diff

Some days passed very slowly, and others went fairly quickly, it didn't make much difference though I still felt I had been in hospital for ever. It was about this time I had to start going for various x-rays, the first one was for a CT scan, like the one that I had had before my operation. Before you are taken down for the x-ray, you have to put this surgical gown on, then a porter arrived with a wheel chair to take you there, this isn't as simple as you think. I had to push the drip stand in front of the wheel chair, as the TPN had to stay connected to me, then the sister told me I had to take my notes with me, these resembled a large encyclopaedia which she placed on my legs and weighed a ton.

When we arrived at the CT scanning room there were a waiting room full of people, so the porter left me sat in the wheel chair in this draughty corridor, I was sat there for about 45 minutes, by the time it was my turn I was absolutely frozen, I only had that thin surgical gown on. I was taken into the room, and placed on the table. (The scanning machine is a large piece of equipment with a large circular hole in it). The table which you lay on slides through and back again, the nurse then puts a canular into your arm and connects it to a long line. The nurse then tells you when this fluid is pumped into you, you might feel warm, or you might feel like you want to wee, but its only a feeling, and now you have to lie on your back on the table, with your hands over your head. The nurse then leaves the room, and then the table starts to move through the circle. Then the machine starts to make a whirring sound, and then a voice tells you to hold your breath, then the table moves back slowly, when you are out of the circle the voice tells you to breathe normally. This happens a couple of times, then the nurse reappears, gives you the injection that she connected to you earlier, she then leaves you to go through the machine again, the nurse then comes and removes the canular and that's about it.

I was then wheeled back into the corridor and left there until the porter came to take me back to the ward. The amount of time you had to wait depended on how busy the porters were. The longest time I waited in a corridor was 75 minutes.

The next x-ray was to check all my pipe work, this was similar to the CT scan, but this machine was like a big camera, and all the doctors and nurses wore protective aprons. The downside to this one was I had to drink this barium meal over a given time. This stuff is horrid, it tastes like chalk. Given my condition when I drank this stuff, all it did was go straight through into my bag, anyway they did the x-ray and that was that.

Now I was feeling a bit better again, and getting about a bit better. Ms Bronder thought it would be a good idea if I got out of the hospital for a while, so I asked Pauline if she would take me for a ride in the car. Ms Bronder said that would be good for me, a change of scenery, and some fresh air.

You know it's a funny thing, but when you have been in hospital for a long time you get hospitalized, at the beginning the days seemed like weeks, but now with Billy's company and with all the other things going on the time seems to pass a lot quicker. The next day Pauline brought the car to the hospital entrance, she then took me in a wheelchair from the ward to the car, and after a bit of a struggle she managed to get me in the seat. The next problem was the TPN, as we couldn't take the machine that regulated it with us, we had to fasten the bag on to the handle in the roof, and regulate the flow to a small drip on the giving set.

We had a nice run out over the Trough of Bowland; it is very scenic over there, I believe a good amount of it belongs to the Duke of Westminster.

We had a lovely afternoon out. Pauline was frightened that with me not having a stomach wall, (only the bag attached), I might feel car sick. My bag was getting full of liquid and Pauline said she could hear it swishing about some of the time. Pauline had to drive very carefully to avoid all the bumps so it didn't hurt my stomach.

We were on our way back, when I asked Pauline to park at a good viewing point. I don't remember this bit, but Pauline recalled this, these are her words.

Paul said he wanted to look across to the sea, power station, etc. We sat a few minutes then he started to recline the car seat. He laid back and gave a big sigh and closed his eyes saying "that's all I wanted". Wanted what? I started to panic; I honestly thought he'd passed away. His last wish fulfilled. I shook him and shouted. He opened his eyes and smiled. Apparently I said "I'm okay love, just a little tired, let's get back".

I think we had stayed out about a couple of hours, it just felt so good to get out of that place for awhile.

After I had been in hospital for this long, I got to know the sisters and nurses very well, and they got to know my dietary needs. Sometimes there would be a different nurse or a trainee, and they would be asking me what I would like to eat, not knowing I was nil by mouth.

Another thing, more often than not the food trolley would be left outside my room door, (now I know that hospital cuisine isn't noted for being excellent), but when you haven't had anything to eat for a long time, it just smelt so good, it was like torture. I used to ask them to leave it somewhere else, but most of the time it fell on deaf ears, I am sure they did it on purpose, just to wind me up.

A little treat at every meal time, was that the drugs were distributed, your chart was clipped on the bottom of your bed, with everything recorded from the various nurses visits throughout the day. The drugs you had to take were listed in the chart, as they differed from day to day; I also had to have an injection once a day, to stop my blood clotting, the other thing I had to have every day was a nebulizer 4 times a day. (This is an oxygen mask, with a little container that takes a small amount fluid), the mask is then put over your mouth and nose, then connected to the oxygen, and switched on. You have to breathe through this until all the fluid disappears. The other things that were recorded on the chart were, your entire intake, and your output, and all your observations.

The nurses on the night shift were also extremely nice, but they also were under a great deal of pressure, as there were a lot less nurses on the night shift than there was on the day shift.

Before you went to sleep, a drink and a biscuits would be brought (but not in my case), they would also give you your medical requirements, do your observations, and bed you down for the night. I was quite lucky in one sense that I knew one of the night nurses indirectly, she was called Janet. I knew Janet through her husband Alan, he worked at one of the firms I sold too when I had my business.

Janet used to come to see me after she had got all the other patients bedded down to see if I was okay. If I was still awake or having trouble getting to sleep, she would bring me a cup of tea or a glass of milk, to try to settle me down, when I was able to eat and drink.

Just another little problem, being on my own in my room I was often forgotten about, sometimes it would have got to about 11pm and I hadn't been seen to yet. So I had to ring the nurse call to get a nurse to come and attend to me.

Other times I would be watching a film or something very interesting on the television, and just at a crucial part, or just before the end, the nurse would arrive, asking all sorts of questions, and how your day had been, the film had ended, or you had lost the jist of it.

I suppose these were all the trials and tribulations of being in hospital for a long time.

Now I don't know how it happened? But there was another set back just round the corner, I contacted the killer bug called C Difficile, known as C Diff. It was probably a good thing I was in my own room at that time, as I was basically put in quarantine. The door had to be kept closed all the time, there was a sign placed on the outside of the door, to alert people entering my room.

Everyone had to wash their hands thoroughly, on entering and leaving the room.

This C Diff thing lasted a few weeks, but before I managed to get rid of it, a sample was taken out of my bag every other day, and sent for testing. Also the microbiologist got involved again to find the right antibiotic to cure this problem.

I was beginning to think I was fighting a loosing battle, as every time I was getting a bit better, (BANG) something else knocked me for a six, and I am back in bed for a week or two. By the way I have still got my bed sores, and the lady doctor still kept arriving with that bowl and large syringe, to empty my back passage, it just gets better, doesn't it?

One thing that struck me as being out of order was, I had been allocated my own blood pressure monitoring machine, and observation equipment. But one day one of the other machines on the ward must have broken down. Mine was taken to use, and never returned. After that the issue of quarantine went out of the window. This was mentioned to the nurses, but nobody seemed to take any notice.

CHAPTER SEVEN

Line Infection No. 2

After recovering from C Diff, things started to look up again, and I was getting about again. I would make my way into the other part of the ward where Billy was, there was a lot more going on in there.

I remember a young boy, about 16 who had been in a car accident, and he had received a serious head injury. His accident had been a lot earlier in the year, and he had been brought to our ward to convalesce. He couldn't remember anything, and he didn't even know his family when they came to visit. He used to walk up and down the ward all day long, he was like a caged animal, when he looked at you, he looked wild. As he got slightly better he started to leave the ward and pace round the hospital, and it wasn't too long before he started leaving the hospital. Many times a doctor or a nurse would bring him back. I remember one time a visitor brought him back, and he got very abusive with her. I remember another time he slapped one of the nurses across the face, and a few times the police brought him back. Pauline once caught him running out of the main entrance of the hospital, shortly followed by a male nurse. Pauline shouted to him to attract his attention, he looked at her and dropped his mobile phone. He had to stop to pick it up, that gave the nurse time to apprehend him. After this confrontation Pauline was advised to keep clear of him, as a female nurse who came to help was knocked down a flight of stairs.

To stop him leaving they took his trousers and shoes off him. They thought that would stop him but the police picked him up one hour later in the middle of Lancaster, no shoes or pants on.

He was a constant problem for awhile, another time he was found about 3 miles away from the hospital, in his pyjamas.

It all helped to relieve the monotony; but as he got his memory back he started to help the nurses, giving out food and other odd jobs.

Another time a prisoner from Lancaster Prison was brought in for a minor operation. Pauline was the first person with the news, it happened that Michala was visiting with the children, and Maddie was kicking off, so Pauline took her out for a while. When she got to the door of the ward there were about 4 people with a trolley, so she opened the door for them. The guy on the trolley gave her a wink, she didn't realize that the men with the trolley were prison officers until they had got through the door; she said that the prisoner was a massive fellow chained and handcuffed to the trolley.

As it happened he was in the bed opposite Billy two sticks. He was in hospital for 3 days, and Pauline was right about him being big, he was about 6 feet 8 inches tall; they had him handcuffed and chained to the bed, and two prison officers stayed with him.

With Billy being across from him, he said he felt a bit uncomfortable with him being there, and said he was going to sleep with one eye open. He could also see everything that was going on. Now this big guy had to have an injection, and Billy said he was absolutely scared to death of that needle, and apparently he fainted when the injected him. Billy said he felt much better after they had cuffed him to the bed.

Pauline was a godsend to lots of patients, as sometimes I would have a sleep in the afternoon, and she would go and talk to patients that didn't have a visitor.

The ward I was on was a medical ward, so there was a quick turn round of patients; we used to get a lot of people in for leg and foot amputations. A standing joke we had with them were, when you are better you can hop it.

I remember one time, this chap came in with a squashed foot it was so bad he had to have it amputated. He told us that he worked at the power station and a twenty ton test weight had accidently dropped on his foot. He was down in the dumps, until he saw Billy and me, then he said he didn't feel too bad after seeing us two looking our best, (which wasn't very good), the amount of time we had been in hospital and what we had been through.

The physiotherapist got me walking a lot better, and eventually they got me going up and down a few steps, this was to get me ready to go home. The problem I had was this TPN, as you need a machine to regulate the dose, the hospital wouldn't let you take the machine home. So if I was to be allowed to go home to stay, a firm that supplies the machines for home use had to be found.

On the occasions I was allowed to go home for the day, I had to regulate the flow on the giving set, but I wasn't allowed to use it like this for too long, as it is quite crucial that it is not given too quickly, as it can cause a heart attack.

It had got to the beginning of May now, and I was allowed to come home for odd days, which felt absolutely marvellous. Pauline would come and pick me up from hospital about 10am, and take me back at about 4 30pm.

We seemed to cope at home okay, so it was decided that they would try to get me home, until I could get to Hope Hospital intestinal failure unit.

Now there are specialist firms that supply these machines, and all the things that go with it.

Now I don't think that they had ever sent anyone home with TPN from Lancaster, as they didn't know a company that gave this service.

Eventually they found this company called Klinovia. The next move was that a representative would come to see me at the hospital, with a few other people. It was like a board meeting, in attendance there had to be, Ms Bronder the consultant, the dietician Tim, the ward sister, someone from the community to agree the finance, and Pauline.

It took about 2 weeks to set this meeting up, eventually the day arrived, and 2 people from Klinovia came, armed with a machine like the one I was going have at home.

The system with Klinovia was, they would supply a fridge with a week's supply of TPN, the machine and the giving sets.

So you can imagine there were lots of forms to fill in, consent forms for doctors and from the community to be sorted out, so everything signed sealed and delivered, I thought at last things were looking up.

Then there was a matter of finance, this was a matter for the community trust fund, apparently this comes under a different umbrella than the NHS.

So another week passes by, and still no nearer.

Next problem, a system had to be set up for my blood results to be sent every week to Klinovia, but before they were sent they had to be checked by Ms Bronder. Nothing is ever simple, and we still couldn't get an answer on the funding. After awhile it starts to get you down, every time you think the problem is solved you hit another brick wall.

It just seemed to be all getting sorted out, and (BANG), here we go again, another line infection, only this one was a lot, lot, worse than the last one. I used to go into what they call the rigors, this condition caused you to shiver and shake violently, your temperature rise's to fever pitch, your pulse starts to race, and your blood pressure goes through the roof. As before all the bed clothes are taken off and fans brought to bring your temperature down.

These rigors would last about 30 minutes, and they would happen about every 4 hours. Enter the microbiologist again, he developed an antibiotic to sort this infection out, but I must say he had to have a few attempts before he got it right.

The microbiologist told me that this antibiotic was very strong, and it had to be kept covered as the light affected it. The doctor that connected it was called Ben; he was a young doctor doing his training. When this stuff came he was looking in some books trying to find a bit more about it, and when he connected it he covered it with tin foil so it wouldn't be affected by the light, it certainly looked strange hung there, and it resembled a turkey leg.

This antibiotic was so strong it had to be given very slowly, it was only a small amount but it took about six hours to give the full dose. But before they would give it to me I had have a test dose for about ten minutes, I then had to wait about one hour to see if I had a reaction to it, when it was deemed to be okay the rest of it was given to me.

It took a few attempts to get the right strength of the antibiotic to get it working properly, and it wasn't very pleasant, because after I had been given the dose for about 90 minutes, I would go into the rigors again, I think that this happened about three or four times before they got the strength right.

You know it takes weeks to get over these infections, not to mention the TPN having to be fed through canular's into my arm again. By this time trying to find a good vein to put the canular in was becoming a real problem.

Eventually the infection had been cured; you've got it, another trip to the theatre for another main line, this time back into the left hand side of my chest.

Pauline and I were getting very fed up by now, and started to pester Ms Bronder every time we saw her about me getting to Hope, or for someone to come from Hope to give a second opinion. Pauline even offered to pay for me to be taken there, but the only answer we got was, you are getting nearer the top of the list, and it shouldn't be long before I would get there.

This line infection had put pay to me getting home with all this equipment from Klinovia, it seemed a shame that all the effort which had been put into getting things sorted out for me to get home, had to be scrapped, but anyway onwards and upwards.

It was the end of May by now, and the weather was getting better, so Pauline used to put me into a wheel chair, and push me into the gardens for a bit of sunshine, and some fresh air. It must have looked funny to passers by, as I was sat in the sun in my wheelchair with my TPN on the drip stand, covered with a bag to stop it getting warm.

I didn't care at least I was getting out of this hospital. I remember one day it was quite breezy, so Pauline found a sheltered spot, underneath the windows of the corridor that lead to the operating theatre. When we got back inside to the ward, loads of doctors and nurses kept asking me if I had got a good suntan, it seemed like half the hospital had been on that corridor that day.

As the days passed, I became well enough to be able to go home again for the odd day or two.

Please forgive me, I have not mentioned Billy two sticks for awhile, we still spent quite a lot of time together, but the funny thing was, when I was in good order, Billy seemed to take a turn for the worse, and when Billy was in good order I would be laid up.

Well Billy seemed to be getting a lot better now, so he was sent home to convalesce. I was a bit sad to see Billy go home, as we had become really good friends, (by the way when eventually I did get out of hospital, we kept in touch, and visited each other at home). Also Billy decided that after living with Lyn for 20years or more that it was time they got married, so Pauline and I were invited to the wedding, which we duly attended and I should say what a fantastic day we had.

Well back to the matter in hand. The new pharmacy they were building outside, was coming on a treat now, so it struck me, how sad is it when the most interesting thing in your life, is the new building outside your room window.

CHAPTER EIGHT

Intensive Care

I was starting to walk a lot better now, so for a change Pauline would occasionally take me to the shops with her. The only problem was, I had to be kept connected to my TPN, so we used to switch the valve off on the giving set, put the TPN into a bag for me to carry. The funny thing is that the bag Pauline found me had printed on it, Bag for Life, which I thought was quite amusing, and very appropriate, the only thing though was, she said I looked like Roy Cropper out of Coronation Street, walking about with my bag.

Talking about bags! Another bag we took with us in the car on our trips out was, an emergency kit, containing a large container, a bottle of water, a kitchen roll, and a packet of sterile wipes. The bag we used for this was a bag we had got with a new vacuum cleaner and it had Henry printed on it. We kept the emergency kit with us all the time, as I never knew when my wound management bag would need emptying, and trust me it was never at a convenient time. Also it had to be emptied quite regular because if it got too full the green bile would melt the adhesive and the bag would come off. So the kit we always carried with us was always referred to as Henry.

It was early June now, and I had been home for three separate days of that week. I remember one day it was a Sunday and Derek and Denise came up for the day, they had a meal with us, although I couldn't eat anything it was nice to sit at the table with them like old times. As Pauline would come and pick me up in the morning, and take me back at tea time, it was a nice change for her when Derek offered to take me back on his way home. The next week I had spent a couple of days at home and I was feeling as good as I had been for a long time, but the big fellow upstairs must of thought, that's enough of that.

On the Saturday the 10th of June I had to stay in bed, as I didn't feel too good, I had a few visitors, it always seemed to be busy at the weekend with visitors, and then on Sunday afternoon I was rushed on to the intensive care unit, with fungal pneumonia. This was when the lights really went out. Pauline and my daughter were visiting at this crucial time. To their amazement, Sister Ann-Marie gave them my case reports and a mobile oxygen cylinder to carry. There was no time to wait for a porter, so the three of them ran pushing me in the bed to the ICU unit; I don't know at what point I was connected to a life support machine, but when Pauline arrived to visit on Monday morning she was told I was on life support, and things didn't look good. This was a lovely present for Pauline, as it was our 35th wedding anniversary on this day, and there she had to call my daughters, Michala and Natalie, to tell them I was on life support, and to get to the hospital as quick as possible as they didn't hold out much hope.

At this point I don't remember a thing, so this next part is Pauline's input.

It is very frightening to be taken for the first time, by the allocated nurse to the bedside. You have to wait for Paul's nurse to come, and tell you what to expect, then taken to this alien place. It's full of monitors, wires, with alarms or bells going off, and patients lying with pipes in every orifice.

As I approached Paul I was told to touch him and speak to him. What do you say? I was practically by the side of Paul when an alarm started peeping on his monitor. You can imagine the panic I had. An entire river cascaded in my inside. Shock horror! I turned for help, only to see a nurse flip a switch and smile at me. Evidently, even though Paul was unconscious, he had recognised my voice and sent wave patterns to the monitor to alert the nurse he wasn't entirely "out of it". I was to find this to be a regular occurrence in the next few weeks, each time Paul was unconscious, his means of telling or contacting me, to tell me he was aware I was there, he set the monitor alarm off. I was asked if I would like to lye in bed and cuddle him, this upset me very much as I had heard that the only reason for this was that the person you were going to cuddle was near the end. So I declined the offer to do this. I thought in my own mind if I get in bed with Paul he would give up his fight for life, I think I did the right thing as he came back to me. I was offered this option three times altogether whilst Paul was on ICU at this time.

That was Pauline's explanation of my first week or so on ICU; I must say she found it very hard and very upsetting to put this part into words.

I was on life support for five days, and you know it's a funny thing, that being on the intensive care unit is the finest place in the world, when you are at deaths door, and you are out of it so to speak, but it is the worst place in the world, when you have come round, and you know what's going on.

That first week on this unit I must have been hallucinating. The stupid things I saw, all the beds looked like fronts of cars, the other patients looked to be wearing fancy dress, and one night I thought they had brought two hells angels on to the ward dressed in all their biker gear.

Eventually after I had been in there about a week I came round a bit, it all seemed very strange, it was like I was floating on a cloud, and nothing seemed real. People talking and other noises all blended into one, it is very hard to explain what it was really like, but after awhile things started to sink in, this is when it hits you that you must have just been to hell and back.

You hear people talk about a near to death experience, and the light at the end of a tunnel, but I must admit that never happened to me, so I can only think I wasn't as near to death as everybody thought.

Back to life on the ICU and it was about now I found I had a tracheotomy in my throat. There were wires connected to every part of my body, and at the back of the bed head was a bank of clocks, monitors, bottles of fluids, and all sorts of other things.

After a week or so thing were looking up but the problem I had was, I wasn't well enough to be moved off the intensive care unit, and be taken to the ward.

At other hospitals they have a High Dependency Unit; so patients in my condition would be taken there until they were well enough to go onto the ward.

Here in Lancaster they don't have such a unit, so here I was laying in bed watching people dying all around me; this seemed to be a common occurrence. I think there were eight deaths in that second week I was on this unit, it's a bit upsetting. You begin to think is it me next?

At this particular time it was the football world cup. Now I am not a football fan, but I think that ninety-five percent, of the people that worked in the intensive care unit were. So when there was an important match on the television, all these televisions appeared from all over the place.

At that time in my life I couldn't have cared less what I was watching, as long as it took my mind of the surroundings.

I don't know, but if you are not familiar with people with a tracheotomy, you are not able to speak, so it made communicating with my visitors very awkward, (not that I had many visitors in there). On the intensive care unit only close relatives were allowed to visit. So to communicate I was trying to write messages down which were nonsense, I didn't seem to be able to write much at all, every time I tried it just looked like a spider had crawled all over the page with ink on its feet, it was all very frustrating to say the least. It seemed like I'd had this tracheotomy for ever, and the days just seemed like weeks when you are just laying there with nothing to do. The only thing to do was watch everybody come and go. They brought a guy into the bed on my right, sort of facing me, (some one had just died in that bed about four hours before), and he seemed to be an okay sort of guy when he came in, but that soon changed, boy did he get awkward. He had to wear an oxygen mask all the time, or should I say he was supposed to. As soon as they put it on he used to rive it of, he used to shout and bawl at the doctors and nurses. He said they were trying to kill him, he struggled with a nurse one day that much that he fell out of bed, and they had to bring a medical lift to put him back in bed. I believe he had been brought from Barrow in Furness hospital, I'll bet they were glad to get rid of him from there. I think they must have injected him with something after his escapade, he certainly went quite.

In the next bed to him was a lady, she was no problem, she just slept all the time, I don't think I ever saw her awake.

Whilst I had my tracheotomy in a friend of Pauline's was brought on to the ICU with pneumonia, she also had to have a tracheotomy fitted, so not only was Pauline visiting me, but visiting Debbie too. My communication with Debbie was a wave across the ward.

A constant problem in there was the alarms that went off all the time. These alarms are to alert the nurses if anything goes wrong, they are connected to different censers on your body, so if something goes wrong the alarm starts to beep. The most usual one to cause a problem, was the one on the end of your finger to record your pulse, this would get knocked off regularly. These alarms just got on your nerves, especially at night; you were just dropping off to sleep, and BEEP, BEEP, BEEP.

Eventually the doctor took my tracheotomy out, it felt great being able to talk again, I had to wear an oxygen mask all the time now, but at least when Pauline came to visit, I could take it off and tell her all about my day, and all the things that had happened on the ICU, all the deaths, that sort of thing you know.

That evening there was an important football match on the television, England against someone, I can't remember. Well it was about half way through and I started to go off a bit, well to tell the truth, I was that bad the doctor thought I was going to die. So I was rushed into the operating theatre, another tracheotomy fitted, the main line in my chest was removed, this was the problem it had become infected, so another one was put in the other side.

Well here we go again, back to square one, but at least I was in the right place, the ICU.

Eventually after a few days I felt a lot better, and after the tracheotomy had been removed for the second time, I asked the doctor about the new line he had fitted, I said I didn't think you could put a line straight back in, he said it was a case of having to, or I would have died.

Anyway all the doctors and nurses on the ICU were all very nice, and I was pleased to find that Godzilla had left, remember her from my last visit to ICU; well I think she must have been sent Guantanamo Bay to torture the prisoners.

Now can you remember me telling you about the bed sores? Well they were getting really bad now, and very painful, so I complained bitterly about these, so they said they would try to get me different bed. About four days later a new bed arrived, when the bed arrived I was told in was the BMW of beds. It was remote controlled which allowed you to adjust the pressure on your bum, and the mattress was filled with air, it was a marvellous bed.

Now it never rains but it pours; I had only been the new tenant of this bed for about three days, and this particular day I felt well enough to be able to be got out of bed, and put into the chair for a while. I must have fallen asleep and when I awoke I found my bed was missing, I asked a nurse where it had gone, she said a new firm had got the bed contract, and all the beds had to be returned to the old contract firm. A while later another bed was brought, a standard one like the old one I had before, and back to the bad bum syndrome.

I was still not eating anything, I think it had been about two months since any food had passed my lips, I was able to drink a little though, I was still having my dioralyte's and I was allowed to have the odd drink of *Lucozade sport*, this was good because my mouth used to get so dry, it was a real treat to have something tasty in your mouth. Being on ICU all this time was sending me stir crazy, and every day I kept pestering Dr Bird about getting back to the ward, he just kept telling me I wasn't well enough to go back yet.

Dr Bird was the doctor in charge on the ICU; he even overruled Ms Bronder when she said she thought I would be better off on the ward, so there it was, I was stuck there for awhile yet.

There were other doctors on the ICU ward, they were Dr Grainger and Dr Tilley, they seemed more approachable and friendly, and took time to explain things to me. Pauline spent a lot of time talking to the doctor's, I think she pestered them quite a bit to see if they could help to get me to Hope Hospital, but they told her it was Ms Bronder's decision, as I was in ICU for my fungal pneumonia and not my fistulas. So I still had to wait for Ms Bronder to get me there.

The days were long, and the nights were even longer, with all the alarms and other noises, patients whaling etc, I just found it so hard to sleep, so I was prescribed a very strong sleeping drug every night, this helped a great deal.

By now Pauline and I were getting cheesed off by all this, it just seemed that nothing was going right, and

Pauline kept on pestering all the doctors about me getting to Hope. She said she was worried I would be leaving Lancaster in a box, if I didn't get out of here soon.

Well Ms Bronder didn't seem to be helping much, so Pauline said she would get in touch with PALS to see if they could help.

The thing about being in ICU for a while is that you get really fed up, and very depressed, I had no interest in wanting to read a book, or anything else for that matter.

All I used to do was watch the patients coming in and going out, okay a lot of them didn't go out under their own steam, if you know what I mean,(in a box), and that gets you even more down. In fact you never saw anybody that had passed away be taken out of the ward. But you always knew when all the curtains were pulled round for a few minutes, when they were pulled back you would see an empty bed.

Every day starts, first with a bed bath, you are pulled up and down, then over to one side then back to the other whilst you are being washed, when you are all nice and clean, the nice clean bed sheets are put on the bed, so you are rolled over to one side, then the dirty bed sheet are rolled up behind you, then the new sheet laid on the bed behind you, then you are rolled back on to the new sheet, then the other part of the sheet is pulled over the other bit of the bed, you are then rolled back, it sounds complicated but it all works well, although if you are well enough you can sit in a chair while your bed is being changed.

Another problem occurred, my legs swelled to an enormous size, they felt like lead balloons, this was put down to the drugs and steroids that were being pumped into me, also with not being mobile for a long time didn't help. I had to have two pillows put under my feet to raise my legs hoping that would bring the swelling down a bit.

Can you remember that pus, which the lady doctor had to remove from my bottom with that syringe? Well it was getting quite troublesome now. It started to run out of my bum, so I spent a lot of time sat on a bed pan, and when I wasn't sat on a bed pan I had to have my bum padded up. Another thing it smelt absolutely horrible, I don't know whether it was the drugs that they were giving me, or what was causing it, but it wasn't very nice.

A month had nearly past, and I was still here in ICU, but miracles do happen, and on Sunday the 2nd of July I was taken back to my old ward. It wasn't the same room as I was in before, but another side room. I couldn't have cared were they took me, as long as it was away from that place.

Monday lunchtime and Pauline came to see me, she remarked that I didn't look well at all and asked me if any one had been to see me. I said Dr Bird had been earlier in the day, Pauline said she didn't like the look of the main line going into my chest, she said it was a funny colour, so she told a nurse who sent for a doctor. It wasn't very long before Mr Clark arrived, he was gowned up and ready to go into the operating theatre to operate on someone. He took one look at me and he dashed out of the room, a few moments later he returned with a nurse and a trolley full of equipment, guess what, he said the line would have to come out as it was infected. I thought oh no not the ICU again! I was wondering how I could kill myself if I had to go there again, but it didn't come to that. Mr Clark put a canular in my arm and sent for the microbiologist again. Here we go again those dam rigours; anyway he got me on the antibiotics quickly this time. Mind you it was getting to too regular occurrence for my liking.

Pauline got really mad and upset; she said something had to be done now it was just getting past a joke, so she started to form a letter of complaint about not being able to get to Hope Hospital. She had also been in contact with PALS, they are there to help sort out any complaints and concerns that patients have with the NHS. PALS, is an abbreviation for the Patient Advice Liaison Service. Pauline had also been in contact with Hope to see if I was on the waiting list.

The next thing was to see my consultant, Ms Bronder, but she was on holiday until Thursday. So Thursday morning first thing Pauline was at the hospital armed with an A4 sheet of paper full of concerns and complaints.

Ms Bronder usually came on her rounds about eight thirty to nine am every morning, but of course she never turned up that morning, so Pauline asked the sister to contact her to tell her she wanted to see her. We waited all day. The sister kept trying her pager but she wasn't answering, eventually at four thirty pm she arrived with Mr Clarke. Staff Nurse Brenda also came into the room to give Pauline some support. Now when Pauline had had concerns before and confronted Ms Bronder she had edged her way out of the room whilst answering the questions, so when she came into the room Pauline closed the door, and stood at the back of it so she couldn't escape. Well Pauline gave her both barrels telling her she was going to put a complaint in about her and everything that had gone on, she said that I couldn't stand much more, and that if I was here much longer I would be leaving in a coffin. At this time the VAC PAC concern was mentioned, and the fact that Brenda was not happy about applying it to an open bowel. Brenda agreed this was the case to Ms Bronder's dismay. Evidently when Brenda left the room, Ms Bronder reprimanded her over this issue. Ms Bronder said that she was in constant contact with Hope. Pauline asked how often constant was, she said once every two to three weeks. At this point Pauline hit the roof and told her she should be ringing every day when I was so ill, and she hadn't a clue what to do with me. I wasn't very well at the time but I did manage to say I was fed up with being her guinea pig. Then Ms Bronder tried to get that piece of paper off Pauline, but Pauline said that if nothing was done by Friday she was going to present this complaint to the authorities. Pauline said that she would give her until Friday lunchtime to sort something out.

Friday morning about nine thirty, Ms Bronder sent a message, telling me there would be a place at Hope for me early next week, it just goes to show what a bit of pressure can do. Pauline said if she had known that was all it would take, she would have gone down that avenue, weeks before.

Monday morning about eight thirty on the tenth of July, Pauline was with me when the sister came into my room and told us there would be an ambulance here about eleven thirty am to take me to Hope. So Pauline had to go back home to get some clothes together, and sort things out at home as she was going to stay at Natalie's, our daughters house, as she lives in Manchester.

Morecambe is about seventy miles from the hospital at Manchester, so it was going to be much better for Pauline to be living close. Pauline arrived about eleven am to go with me in the ambulance, but true to form the ambulance was delayed, and didn't arrive to pick up until about three thirty pm, but they soon had me on the trolley and off to the ambulance. After a quick goodbye to all the staff on the ward, I was off into the unknown and away from the nightmare.

CHAPTER NINE

Where there's Hope there's Salford Royal

The ambulance didn't seem to take long to get to Hope Hospital, probably it didn't seem long as I was asleep most of the way, due to the fact that I was very ill. So when I got there I was admitted straight on to the High Dependency Unit. Having never been on a High Dependency unit before I didn't know what to expect, it was very similar to the ICU from what I could make out.

The difference mainly between ICU, and HDU, is that on ICU each patient has their own nurse, and on HDU one nurse has two patients. But to be honest I don't think this was the case at Lancaster ICU.

I had brought all my medical records with me from Lancaster, you should have seen the thickness of the folder, I bet it would have taken a week to read them all from cover to cover. Luckily everything that had happened to me had been condensed on to about six pages.   I was connected to all sorts of monitors to check my condition. It was later that evening that I met Professor Carlson, he was the consultant I would be under, and hopefully the chap that could sort me out. He asked me if was eating anything, I told him I was only having the dioralyte's, and the odd drink of *Lucozade sport*. He had a look at my fistula's, then he told me that if I wanted a cup of tea, and something light to eat, it would be okay as it wouldn't affect what he was going to do in the slightest, he said these fistula's would never heal up, and would have to be cut out eventually.

I think they had been in touch with Lancaster to find out about the antibiotic they were giving me, to combat my line infection. Different people kept arriving to take blood and do other tests. Then a nurse arrived with the antibiotic and connected me up, I think there must have been something slightly different with the one they were giving me, to the one I'd had in Lancaster. It had only been running for a short while, and I started with the rigors, but it didn't take them long to get the mix right.

I think I was on HDU for a couple of days before things started to happen.

The next two days were none stop. I cant remember how many tests and x-rays I had in those two days, but I don't think I covered this many miles on a trolley all the time I was in Lancaster, as I had covered in these two days.

Hope is a huge hospital in comparison with Lancaster. The x-ray departments seemed to be miles away, as soon as I got back to the HDU from one x-ray I was off again for another. Another thing that was different here there was no waiting about in draughty corridors; it was straight to the department, into the x-ray, job done then straight back to the HDU. Another difference was the amount of x-rays. At Lancaster you might have had one or two, here you had more like twenty two, and they x-rayed you in every angle possible. I can't remember how many different types of x-rays I had, but I sure had a lot.

After about three days on HDU they put me in a room of my own within the HDU unit. The staff were very good and very attentive towards me, and they soon had me ready for the ward, I think I was only on HDU for about two weeks altogether. From there I was taken to ward B2. The ward I was trying to get on to was B4, which was the intestile failure unit. So when I was taken to the ward I was given my own room, I was getting a bit paranoid about this, as every ward I went to I was found my own room I was beginning to think I must have a very contagious disease or something, but really it was the only bed available at the time.

B2 was a medical ward, and I was told I was only there until there was a bed available on B4. The problem with getting on to B4, was that most of the patients needed to be there for a long time, to get prepared to be able to go home. It was okay on B2; I had a television to watch to help pass the time, as the visiting hours were down to two hours in the afternoon, and two hours in the evening, which was a bit of a blow, as Pauline had spent a lot of time with me at Lancaster.

A funny thing but that horrible smelly stuff that was coming out of my bum had stopped, and the funny feeling had stopped as well. I still had my bum sores but the nurses were taking care of them better here, some super cream and a dressing, I felt a lot better already.

While I was on this ward I seemed to have a lot of trouble with the wound management bag on my stomach. I think a lot of the trouble was that the staff on the ward wouldn't let Pauline change it, and they didn't have the time to spend on fitting it properly, so a few times they had to send for a nurse from B4 to come and do it. The nurses from B4 were very competent at this, as they were fitting them all the time on their ward. I told the staff on

B2 if they let Pauline do it, it would save a lot of bother, but it fell on deaf ears.

    I remember one day this male nurse called Angelo was looking after me, it was early on in the morning and I told him my bag needed changing as it was leaking. He seemed to be very busy, so I said if he was too busy I could ring Pauline, and she would come and put a new bag on for me. He said not to worry, he would do it when he had time, I'll bet you can't guess? Well he never did get time, and by the time Pauline arrived in the afternoon, I was wet through. I had padded myself up the best I could, but I was still covered in all this rubbish out of my bag, and of course all the bed needed changing. So Pauline changed my bag and helped me get cleaned up, all's well that ends well. I don't know why it was happening, but I didn't seem to be able to keep a bag on my body, for longer than a day whilst I was on that ward. Another time when Angelo was looking after me, and I needed a bag change early morning, surprise, surprise, he rang Pauline, to see if she could come in and change it for me.

    It's a funny thing, but now I was on this ward, the two minutes thing started to happen again, I think it must be the first thing the nurses are told to say in their training. It was while I was on this ward that I was told the fungal line infection had been cleared up, but on one of the x-rays some blood clots on my lungs had shown up, so there was some concern that their might be some round the back of my heart. The next thing to happen was to try and find out if there were any blood clots anywhere else. One day a doctor arrived at my room with a big machine and a couple of nurses, he told me he needed to put this camera down my throat, to see if there were anything around the back of my heart. The good news was every thing was clear.

It was a surprise to me, that by putting a camera down your throat, they could see at the back of your heart.

I couldn't fault them at Hope, on how meticulous they were in trying to find out if everything was clearing up. As the next few months passed, I seemed to have every test, and x-ray under the sun, which I will explain in more detail later on in the book. Back to the bag problem, and I think I had had two or three bags on, on this particular day. So a nurse from B4 came to our assistance, she was a black nurse, and she had a fantastic sense of humour. I got to know her well when I eventually got on to B4. When she started to fit a new bag, she said have you tried suction? We didn't know what suction was. This involved connecting the suction pipe to the outlet of the bag, so it could suck all the bile out while the adhesive on the bag set on my body, I had to smile, because as she was fitting it she said in a husky voice, (I just love suction).

CHAPTER TEN

B4 - My new home for the next few months

It wasn't too long before I was transferred to B4, about two weeks or so. Hopefully things could only get better now that I had got to where I wanted to be. I was taken from one ward to the other by a porter, who pushed me there in my bed. Pauline followed with all my personal bits and pieces. I didn't know anything about the ward B4, only it was for intestile failure, and all the patients on there are in a similar situation as me. I was quite surprised to find it wasn't very big, there were only thirteen beds altogether, two large rooms with five beds each in, and three single rooms. And I am led to believe that there are only two such wards in the country, one in London, and this one at Hope. This gave me an idea of why I had to wait so long to get a bed on here. I was wheeled into one of the larger rooms; the bed at the bottom right had the curtains round it, and the other three beds were occupied by ladies. I remarked that I had been taken on to the wrong ward, as they were all ladies, I was pushed into the bottom left, facing the bed with the curtains round, I was pleased to see there was a man in the bed when the curtains were pulled back, apparently the beds are in such demand on this ward, the rooms have to be mixed. And also there was a lot more ladies than were men on the ward. The guy that occupied the bed opposite was called Kevin; he was good company, and a great guy. Its funny though, there is always someone worse than yourself, and poor Kevin had been in hospital for seventeen months. Not only had he got fistulas, but he only had one leg, and his only foot was all swollen and had gone a funny colour. I think also he had a lot of other complications. He used to make me laugh, because every evening he would open his locker drawer, and you would hear these bottles jingle, and out would come the whiskey bottle. He always had a glass or two every evening. His wife Joan didn't visit that much due to certain circumstances, and being quite disabled, but when she did visit she always brought a bag full of quarter bottles of whisky. I don't know if he was supposed to have alcohol, but I think because he had been there that long the nurses turned a blind eye to it.

The names of the three ladies on the ward were, Mary, Wendy and Maureen. Mary arrived at about the same time as I had, but the other two had been there for awhile. They were all very nice, but the sad thing is all the other four people on that ward were still there when I went home in October.

B4 was a completely different ward than any that I had been on, from the first day of arriving there; you were encouraged to look after yourself as much as possible.

And as most patients were there for a long time, it was made as much like home as possible. There was a washing machine, our own fridge, tea and coffee making facilities. You were also encouraged to take charge of your own drugs, and all your fluid records, which had to be all weighed and logged. We also had a television each at the bottom of the bed. These televisions were suspended from the ceiling so you had to have the volume fairly loud, this caused a bit of a problem if you were watching a different program, and you had to keep adjusting the volume so you could hear it. This caused a bit of a problem sometimes, so a nurse would arrive and make us turn them down. To combat this problem I asked Pauline if she could find a pair of headphones with a very long lead, she got some from Argos, problem solved. I think the best thing was, there was no visiting hours, so friends and relatives could come and go at any time of the day. I was encouraged to eat more now, this resulted in my wound management bag filling up a lot quicker, but on this ward they had a solution for this problem, it was called a Megostomy. This was a threaded plastic tube with plastic nuts that went into the spout on the bottom of my wound management bag; the nuts screwed the bag tight to the tube and the same into some lay flat tube, which went into a two and a half litre container. The only problem with this was, my bag was larger than the plastic tube was designed for, so it leaked a bit, but with a bit of messing, and a lot of tape I could get it to stop leaking.

It wasn't until I got to Hope that I realised why I kept getting the line infections. The first thing was, where the giving set is connected to the pipe that comes out of your body, it is always covered with a sterile patch, but at Lancaster it was just left to dangle, usually near the wound on my tummy. Then when the nurses changed your line, it was more like an operation, than at Lancaster it was just a casual, screw this one off, and screw the new one on. The first time I watched them change a line at Hope I was gob smacked. I will explain the procedure to you; the first thing was that the nurse scrubbed their hands and arms for about five minutes. Then the trolley was prepared, that was washed then wiped with a sterile cloth, then a line changing sealed kit was opened on the top of the trolley. A sheet of sterile paper spread on the top of the trolley, and then the contents of the kit were spread out in order with a pair of plastic tweezers on to the sterile paper. Everything was covered with another sheet of sterile paper until it was time for the giving set to be removed, or connected.

When it was time for the procedure the nurse in question washed their hands and arms meticulously. The trolley was pushed to the bed, not with hands as you would think, but it was pushed with their feet. The nurse then rubs some gel on their hands, and then the first pair of sterile gloves was put on, then out of the kit some fluid was poured out of a bottle into a tray. A piece of sterile paper is fastened on to your body, so the line coming out of your body does not touch your skin, so there is no contamination. The connector is then uncovered, and dabbed with the fluid out of the tray with cotton wool; a pair of tweezers is used for this operation. The connector is then uncoupled, there is a one way valve inserted here, this is changed twice a week, the nurse then removes their gloves, more gel applied, then a new pair of gloves are put on. If the line is not going to be connected back to the giving set, the end of the connector is dabbed with the fluid, and then an injection of an anticoagulant is put down the line. The nurse then does a glove change again; the line is then folded up in a sterile dressing, and then fastened to your body where the line comes out.

I forgot to mention that where the line comes out of your body, this also gets a good dabbing with the fluid. If they are connecting the line back to the giving set, then all the joints on the connectors are well dabbed before they are joined back together, then it is wrapped in a sterile dressing and fastened to your body. So you can probably see, like me, why I ended up with so many line infections at Lancaster.

Also on this ward the nurses changed the TPN on other patients that weren't on this ward, when it was time for them to have it done a porter would bring them in a wheelchair, then take them back after.

There was also a training room for patients that were going to be on TPN permanently to learn how to do it for themselves. In the room there was a dummy to practice on, and I can tell you it took a long time for anyone to get proficient enough to be able to go home and look after the TPN themselves. This was one thing I was getting a bit worried about, (would I have to be on TPN for the rest of my life).

With having so many line infections, I was unable to have a new line put back in my chest, so it was decided that a line would be put in the top off my arm. This is called a pick line. This was done about a week after I had gone onto B4, and this involved a small operation. I was taken to an x-ray room to have this done, presumably to see if the line had gone into the right place. This line goes into a vein in your arm above the elbow, this is a thin plastic tube which is pushed up your vein, and it stops just short of you heart. This line is pushed in not by hand, but with a machine, I think this is why the x-ray is quite crucial. Well when it's all done a connecter is fastened on the end of the line, so the TPN can be fed through it. Now I had got my new pick line, the TPN could be fed overnight at a faster rate, instead of me having to have it for twenty four hours a day. This was a great relief to me; this was the first time in months I could walk around on my own, without that dam drip stand. I felt I was like a prisoner being released from a ball and chain.

Whilst I was on B4 Professor Carlson used to call to see me periodically. Of course there were the usual daily ward visits by the doctors every morning. It was decided that I had to go for many tests, and x-rays, with having contracted blood clots on my lungs in Lancaster. I had to go for a breath test, this test took about seven hours to complete. On the day of the test I was taken to a room, at the other end of the hospital. In that room were four other people, we were given some fluid to drink, the nurse said it was very dangerous, but I can't remember for my life what she said was in it. After I had drunk this stuff, I had to breathe into a container which collected my breath, every fifteen minutes for one hour, then every thirty minutes for three hours, then every hour for three hours. I also had to go for another CT scan, and various x-rays for one thing or another. I even had to go for an ultra sound examination; this is when gel is rubbed on your body, and the camera is moved gently on your body, you know, like the one that ladies go for when they are pregnant, to see the baby. I new I couldn't be pregnant so it must have been for another reason.

As I was feeling much better again, and free from my ball and chain so to speak, Pauline would take me out in my wheel chair, we would go and sit in the gardens if the weather was nice, or sometimes we would go out in the car. She also took me to the Lowry Outlet Village, the War Museum, and to the Trafford Centre. After all these months it was great to go somewhere different, Pauline said she would look like a muscle man by the time she had finished pushing me about. I must say though, how well these places are equipped for the disabled person, the provision of wheelchairs, and the help of the staff was impressive, this was a great help to me as I was unable to walk more than ten steps at a time.

I remember Pauline once took me to a large B&Q store; I was sat in my wheelchair and behind me was a forklift truck reversing, it's reversing bleepers were sounding which immediately caused me to put my hands over my ears, Pauline shouted at me saying I looked like a retard, I couldn't help it, it so reminded me about ICU.

The visitor situation was getting good too; my daughters and their husbands, and my grandchildren came to see me weekly. Derek and Denise still came to see me once a week, Pauline's sister Kathryn and her husband Graham were also weekly visitors. Now I was in Manchester I had a lot of visitors from round that area that came on a regular basis.

Do you remember Pete, the person who tripped over my catheter when I was in Lancaster? He and his wife Sue lived on the outskirt of Manchester, so when Sue was well enough, they would come and visit. Sue had cancer, sadly she passed away in two thousand and seven, shame really she was a very nice person and a real character.

Well back to the plot, after I had been on B4 for a while, the concern was to sort out my fistulas, so I was sent for another x-ray called a fistula gram. This was to measure the distance, and the proximity, of the fistulas in my small bowel. I had to lie on my back on the bed in radiology, and a pipe with a catheter on the end was pushed down each fistula. There were five in all. The bulb on the catheters was then inflated so they wouldn't come out, then fluid was put down the pipe with a syringe, in order. Then it was x-rayed in order to measure the distance of each fistula in the bowel. One of the reasons this was done, was to ascertain the amount of good bowel I would be left with. During the examination when the doctor did the bottom fistula, he seemed quite pleased with the result, he commented that the fluid went down towards the large bowel, and there was a possibility that they could feed me through the bottom fistula, into my large bowel. I was told that if I was able to be fed this way, instead of by TPN, there would be less chance of infection, this sounded good to me.

Back to the ward, and a few days later and that's what happened. I had a pipe with a catheter on it pushed down my bottom fistula, which went down towards my large bowel. This pipe was then connected to a giving set, to supply me with the food, which is called Perative. This is like a thick milky substance, which is full of nutrients. I had to have one and a half litre of this, and one and a half litre of saline, in a twenty four hour period. This is called distal feeding and things didn't go too well for a while, it seemed that everything that was fed through the pipe came straight through into my stoma bag. It took a good few days for it to start to settle down and to start to work properly. The doctor said that some patients couldn't feed that way for some reason, so you can imagine how relieved I was when my body started to accept the food. You can't believe how relieved I was at the thought not having any more line infections. As I was being fed this way now, it meant that I needed other kinds of nutrients in the form of tablets and powders. The items I needed to keep me going so to speak were, ten sachets of dioralyte, which had to be diluted in water, three sachets of magnaspartate, which also had to be diluted in water, thirty Lopramide, three of these capsules had to be dissolved into a small amount of water, sucked up into a syringe and injected down the pipe into my large bowel, four times a day, six omeprazole, six codeine, and one zinc sulphate tablets, this was my daily intake, and not forgetting my injection of timsaparine, to stop my blood clotting, after the lung scare. Now things were on the right track, and I would have to wait at least six months for my next operation, as my intestines would take at least that long for them to be suitable to be operated on.

While I was on this ward Pauline was encouraged to change my bag and help with other duties, she was told if she could look after me I would get home sooner.

Pauline had got very good at fitting my bag now, she had started to use a hair dryer to dry the area round the wound. After removing the old bag she would remove the residue adhesive with some special fluid, and then wash the area fully, the other thing that she had to do (as I am quite hairy) she would have to shave all the area where my bag would stick, I would then hold some swabs over the fistulas to prevent the stuff running out, Pauline would then dry the area with hair dryer then it was a case of get the bag on as quick as possible. As there wasn't a large area that was adhesive on the bag, Pauline had to put adhesive pads round the edge of the bag, and covered them with a waterproof film so when I showered the bag wasn't dislodged.

The hole in the bag had been cut to size before she started; we had a template the size of my wound so the hole was cut to the right size. This job got a lot more difficult when I started the distal feed. The pipe that fed me had to go through the bag, so a thing called a cone went through the front of the bag which held a rubber diaphragm in place, which was held in place with a plastic cover that clipped on to the cone, and then the pipe went through the centre. I remember one day the doctor came on her visit she had about eight people with her, they were nurses and sisters from other Hospitals in the North West. One of the sisters asked who was fitting my bag, the doctor said it was Pauline, she said it was a good job, and asked if she wanted a job at her hospital fitting them. The longest time I would have a bag on would three days, (if I was lucky), then it would start to get sore where the bile would start eating at the adhesive.

The fistulas were getting very large now, and I thought it was amazing how you could live with half your guts hanging in a bag at the front of you. At the back of the book there is a photograph of my fistulas with the feeding pipe going into the lowest fistula. There is also a photo of my bag with feeding tube.

I had been on this feeding regime for quite awhile now, and the feeding rate had been increased, so instead of having to feed for twenty four hours, my feeding was reduced to twenty hours a day which gave me a four hour period during the day free of my pipe.

As I was coping well with everything the doctor suggested that with the loan of a machine, I might be able to go home for a weekend to see if we could manage okay. This was the best news I had had for months, as it was now late September, and I had been in Hospital for a total of eight months. Well the weekend arrived, and off we go back home, I couldn't wait as it had been four months or more since I been home. It was fantastic to be home, it felt a little strange for a while until I got used to the quietness and the surroundings, and we seemed to be managing fine except for one small hick up. On the Friday early evening when we started to couple the giving set to the pipe, we couldn't find the little screw connecter, which connects the two pipes together, (the nurse had forgot to put one in). Pauline went through to Lancaster Hospital to get one, but to no avail, they had never seen anything like it, so when Pauline got back home, I got into a bit of a panic, so I started to look at it seriously. I found that one pipe was thinner than the other, so one slipped into the other, and with a bit of tape round it, it was fine. It saved having to go back to Hope to sort it out; it certainly put us on our toes to make sure we had all the necessary equipment the next time we came home. As we had coped very well at home that weekend, a meeting was set up with a representative from Homeward. This is a company that supplies the pumps, the giving sets, the bottles, the perative, and the saline, this meeting was to organize everything to be sent directly to my home.

This went so smoothly, not like the meeting we had had at Lancaster, months before, everything seemed to get sorted out in about two weeks. So I think I had four weekends at home, before I came home for good. Pauline would fetch me home on Friday afternoon, and take me back on Monday morning. It was the weekend before I was to be released, and I had been told I could probably go home on Tuesday if every thing was okay, but silly me, I had some avocado pear on the Sunday, and it had put my potassium level high, so I had to stay another week, I didn't make that mistake again!

CHAPTER ELEVEN

Home at Last

So in October I came home, hopefully to get built up for my next operation.

When I arrived home to my surprise Meryl and Norman our next door neighbour's had erected a big sign, saying nine months in hospital and it's a boy. Fastened to the sign and all around the door were about fifty blue balloons. We had lived next door to Meryl and Norman for over twenty years, they had always been good neighbours and over the years we had had many good times.

Before I left the hospital, Professor Carlson said it would be a good idea to try and take a short holiday, so no further ado, Pauline booked a four night stay at a Warner break. This was a Monday to Friday break, at Home Lacy House, near Ross on Wye.

I have a very good friend that lives down in this area of the country, although it was across country, it seemed like a good idea to go and stay with him for the weekend, after leaving the hotel.

I have a friend who lives in Morecambe, who has a mobility shop, so I borrowed a light weight wheelchair off him, to take with us. With all the food, the saline, and all my medical equipment, we had seven quite large cardboard boxes, so you can imagine with our suitcases as well the car was quite full. When we arrived at the Hotel, the porter came to take our luggage to our room. It took him three trips with his trolley.

It just felt great to be away on holiday after nine months in Hospital. The place was fantastic, I had a good time being pushed round the large gardens, and everyone there, were very helpful, and nothing was too much trouble. It was a real change and it did me the world of good. Pauline's cousin Jean, and her husband Peter, live in South Wales, and as we were down at the bottom end of Wales, we thought it would be nice to spend a day with them. So we had arranged to meet them on the Wednesday at Brecon. It's sod's law, on the Wednesday morning just after breakfast my bag started to leak, so we had to get back to the bedroom to put a new bag on. This didn't run smooth, every time Pauline had got everything clean and dry this dam green stuff spouted out, it took about four attempts before we got a new bag on. Eventually when we got there we spent about three hours together; it was nice to see them, as it had been months before, when they had been to visit me in Hospital when I was very ill. The five days at Home Lacy was great, but like all good things it passed too quickly, and it was time to make our journey across Country, to Wolsthorpe in The Vale of Belvoir, near Grantham, to stay with John.

Now the problem we had was with this dam wound management bag and having to empty it on a regular basis. It wasn't a problem when we were on the motorway, as there were a lot of service stations to stop at, but going across country on A roads was a different situation. Trying to find a toilet was almost impossible, so good old Henry the emergency pack came to the rescue. We had to find a quiet lay-by and manage to empty my bag the best I could. In hindsight I should have connected up to a megostomy, if I had I wouldn't have had this inconvenience, not to worry; we can all be wise after the event. We had probably got about half way across country when John rang, and arranged to meet us at Bingham. He wanted to meet us there, so he could take us to the pub he had just recently bought, as it was quite near. It was at a place called Granby, which was on the way to John's house. Eventually we arrived at Wolsthorpe; it had taken quite a long time to come across country due to heavy traffic, I was quite whacked out to tell the truth, and glad to be there, and be able to have a lie down for a while.

John's life hadn't been easy for the last couple of years, as his partner Susan had not long passed away. She had suffered with Motor Neurone disease, and John had given up work to look after her. This really is a terrible disease, she only lived just over a year, after she was diagnosed with it, it really knocked John for a six, but he seems to be coping okay now. We had a great time at John's. He lives in the village which is overlooked by Belvoir Castle; it's a lovely part of the country with lovely views and landscapes. As it happened, it wasn't going to be too long before we were going to be back there for a week or so.

Pauline's Sister's husband Graham was going to a hospital in Huntington, to have two new hips fitted. He was going to be there for two weeks, and as he lived in Mytholmroyd, near Halifax, West Yorkshire, it meant he wouldn't have any visitors, with being so far from home. Graham had been every week to visit me when I was in hospital, I thought it was my duty to go and stay at John's, and to go and visit him daily as it was only about forty five minutes away down the A1. I had grown to know how important it was to have visitors, as he had been so good to me over the last nine months I thought I would return the favour.

Before we went I had an HPN clinic appointment at Hope. I had to go every two weeks to make sure everything was okay, I had to give blood samples, and they would take your muscle mass, and your weight, and see if you were feeding okay, and to check if your output wasn't too excessive. The first time I went, they were a little concerned I had lost a bit of weight, but after the next couple of times I put a little bit on, so instead of having to go fortnightly, they made my appointments monthly. Well off we go back down to Wolsthorpe near Grantham, for our daily visits at Huntington to see Graham, I think it did me good, all this coming, and going. We had a few disasters with my bag, but we got by. There was one funny disaster so to speak, (I will elaborate). Pauline had a nasty fall before we went down to visit, and her leg was swollen, and badly bruised. This particular day, when we got to Huntington, the car park which was next to the toilets were full, so we had to find another one. The one we found had one of those pod toilets, well I had never been in one of these before. I found it was a stainless steel pot with very wide brim, now to empty my bag I have to kneel down, but the floor was wet through, so I tried to be clever and empty it stood up. Well all the stuff that came out of my bag hit the rim of the toilet pot; it came back all over my trousers, what a mess. I was wet through and not smelling too good either, so when we got to Graham's Hospital room I had to take my trousers off and wash them. I borrowed a pair of Graham's track suit bottoms, which were a bit small. I had to put my trousers on the radiator to dry. I was sat there in a badly fitting pair of pants, and Pauline was sat with her legs up on the bed, with her skirt pulled up, when the nurse came in, and gave us a puzzled look. After we gave her a quick explanation, she remarked that Graham was in better shape than his visitors.

We stayed at Johns until three days before Graham was allowed to go home, as I had another clinic appointment at Hope.

Now it was just a matter of time to get built up for my operation, which was to cut out the fistulas, rejoin my bowel back together, and to close the big hole in my abdomen. After a few more visits to the clinic, and as my weight was gaining, my strength, and muscle mass, was getting better, my visits were extended to every three months. There were a few concerns; they found a few deficiencies such as, my vitamin D, which I had to have an occasional injection for. I also had to take three sachets of a magnesium powder a day, as well as all of other tablets I had been prescribed.

Now we had been home for some time and still struggling with this leaky bag, not only did we have disasters when we were out and about, but also there were a few in the middle of the night. I would wake up wet through so I had to get up and shower while Pauline stripped the bed, then of course a new bag had to be fitted. By now Pauline had got more proficient at this bag fitting lark. She found that if she put a new bag on around 12pm to 1am the discharge from my fistulas was very minimal, this helped no end not having to worry about a bowel eruption.

Another thing related to my bag was, I had to kneel down to empty it every time and it played havoc with my knees, I was on my knees that often I got calluses.

So by now Christmas had been and gone, and between Christmas and Easter I had an appointment to see Professor Carlson. This was to talk me over my future operation. He explained all the problems that might occur, and the benefits of the operation. At this time he couldn't give me a date for the operation, but he thought I was recovering quite well, and to just keep attending the clinic. He said he would let me know when he thought I would be ready. Easter had been and gone, and still no word about an operation, so we thought it was time to start pestering someone. The Doctors at the clinic couldn't help; they said it would happen when the Professor thought the time was right. The only person we could get any sense from, was Alison the Professors secretary, who told us it wouldn't happen until the back end of the year.

Another clinic visit, the thing about these visits, they were always followed up by a letter to my GP; I will give you an idea of the contents.

Letter to my GP on 30. 04. 07.

DIAGNOSES.
1. Proximal small bowel fistula secondary to anastomotic leak following resection of Dukes A adenocarcinoma
2. on fistuloclysis

I reviewed Paul in HPN clinic today. I am pleased to say that he is doing very well. He continues to put on weight. He is now 75.4kgs with a BMI of 25.3.he tells me that he is due to be going on holiday to Kefalonia for 5 weeks in the near future. He has been seen by Professor Carlson in his outpatient's clinic, who is waiting for rectal contrast studies with a view to possible surgery.
I am also pleased to say that his epigastric pain that has been troubling him for some time has now completely settled. I plan to review him in a further 4 months. We will keep you informed of his progress.

    Some times after a clinic visit there would be a discrepancy in my bloods, so this meant another short visit to the Hospital for an infusion of some sort. I think I had about four such visits while I was waiting for my operation.
    As things weren't happening very quickly we thought it would be a good idea to go to Kefalonia to see our new Villa, which had now been ready for 18 months.
    Now we had the problem of trying to make the journey. This proved to be a mammoth task, but Pauline booked a return flight for a 5 week period, and we decided that we would cross the next bridge as we came to it. The first problem was to be able to get all the things to keep me living, plus all my wound management equipment over to

Kefalonia. The total amount of weight, of the equipment needed for the 5 weeks was 26 stone. The airline would allow us to take 2 special plastic boxes, called rumble truck, with a maximum weight of 25kg each; these could be taken free if containing life saving equipment. We had our usual luggage allowance, but it still came a long way short of 26 stone.

Our first move was to contact a very good Greek friend, to see if he could arrange the perative food and the saline, from a local pharmacy. These items made up the bulk of the weight, and after many phone calls and faxes, it turned out they could be bought but they would cost a fortune.

As it happened it turned out that the company that supplied my food, giving sets, and bottles, would send it abroad once a year, so that people on intravenous feed could go on holiday. The company kindly dispatched a month's supply, we wouldn't have known of this free service if the delivery guy hadn't mentioned it, (I don't know what we would have done). The next problem was the insurance; every company we rang didn't want to know. But help was at hand again. Down at Hope Hospital they had a list of insurance companies, that other patients had managed to get insurance with, so a couple of phone calls later, and bingo, I had some holiday insurance.

So now with most problems solved, I just needed enough medicines, and wound management equipment, for my 5 weeks away. The flight was booked from mid May and returning in late June. All set to go and just a few little problems of mine to sort out. I could walk a little better now but had a problem with standing and I could only manage a couple of minutes before I had to sit down. So

Pauline booked me a wheelchair at Manchester, and one at Kefalonia. When booking the flight the booking clerk suggested with my condition I was eligible for a medical seat at the front of the plane. My next dilemma was this dam bag that needed emptying on a regular basis. I thought this might be a problem on the plane, so I got a megostomy set up from Hope, to see me on my forward and return journey.

Now the stuff that comes down the pipe into the canister on the megostomy doesn't look very nice, so we had a cover made for the pipe and the canister to hide it.

The day arrived, my daughter Natalie and her husband Michael ran us to the airport, and helped us with our entire luggage. There was me in a wheelchair with my pump in a rucksack, and as it was early morning I was still being fed through my pipe, and the megostomy pipe coming out of my trousers, into the container between my feet, I dread to think what I must of looked like to the other passengers.

On the trolley we had 2 large rumble trucks, and 2 large suitcases, (it's a good job Michael was there to help).

All went well until we had to take the 2 rumble trucks to a different area, because they weren't suitcases. Now you always find one, when they get a uniform on they think they are God. This guy wouldn't send these boxes down the conveyer belt; he said it was more than his job was worth until he had got clearance. We had a list from the Hospital with all the items in the box, which had been signed and cleared by the check-in clerk, (but that wasn't good enough for him), he kept trying to ring someone, eventually he sauntered off up to the other end of check-in area to seek authority, it must have taken him 25 minutes. By the time he got back there was a queue of about 15 people with golf clubs, and packages of all shapes and sizes. So when he got back he must have got his authority and off they went down the chute, and from then on everything ran smoothly, apart from the security guy that had to look under my shirt for security reasons, and on seeing my wound nearly fainted.

At Kefalonia I was wheeled into the airport terminal from the plane by an official at about 50 mile per hour, with Pauline running behind with all the coats and hand luggage. A kind gentleman helped Pauline take all our stuff off the conveyor belt and stacked them on two trolleys. Which were loaded into a taxi and away we went. Just what we both needed a good holiday and we were both thrilled to bits with our Villa.

We were pleased that we had managed to get to our Villa and had a stress and trouble free holiday, it did us both the world of good.

Back home and another appointment to see Professor Carlson, he said that things were looking good for the operation and he would set things in motion for later in the year, I think we were looking at September 2007. I was sent to see Mr Watson (the plastic surgeon at Wythenshawe Hospital). He is the guy that is going to come to Hope to fill the cavity in my abdomen, after the Professor has finished his bowel reconstruction. On my first visit to see him, he asked if we minded if a nurse came and took my bag off so he could see the open wound, to see if the hole could be pulled together. Pauline said she could do it but she would have to go to the car for a new bag and all the equipment that went with it. We always carried a spare bag with us as you never knew when it might come off. After an inspection he said he didn't think it would pull together and it would need some muscle to fill it, he said he could take the muscle from under my arm, by my shoulder, and fasten into my abdomen; he said I would never use this muscle unless I was a rock climber, so that bit sorted then.

After he had finished his inspection he said before you put the bag back on I would like some pictures, so a few minutes later a chap came into the room with a camera, took some photos and left. Funny thing though every time a plastic surgeon came to see me he took photos, I suppose they are to compare different stages.

A few months later and back to see the Professor again, he told me that the he could do the operation early December. But true to form, things don't always seem to go right for me, and after a pre-op and a blood test it appeared that my thyroids had gone underactive, and there was no way he would attempt such a large operation until my thyroids were right. We were playing a waiting game again.

I had to go for my 3 monthly HPN clinic visits down to Hope, your blood was taken by a nurse, and your weight, your muscle mass was taken by the dietician, she also needed to know what you were eating and drinking, and if you were copeing okay with the distal feed. She was very pleased how well I looked, and asked me if I could bring her some pictures of me distal feeding in Kefalonia, she said it might help other patients that weren't copeing very well. There is a picture at the back of the book of me connected to the feed in Kefalonia. The other thing was to talk to the Doctor, and he really just wanted to see if you were copeing okay with everything.

So now I was on more medication, to try and sort this thyroid problem out, the more people I talked to about it, the more despondent I got, as it didn't seem to be very curable. I was told about people that had to have an operation to cure it, the thought of having to have another operation to be able to have another operation, if you know what I mean. So my GP kept increasing the dose, which has to be done slowly over a few months.

So 2007 went by the board, neither was 2008 looking very favourable for my operation.

So a couple of trips out to Kefalonia were in order, one early and one in September. The only problem with this was, Homeward would only send enough food, bottles, and giving sets for one visit, which is only fair, it was good of them to send it anyway.

My delivery from Homeward was every month, and consisted of 90 bottles, 30 giving sets, 30 1ltr and 30 $\frac{1}{2}$ litre bottles of perative, and 90 $\frac{1}{2}$ litres of saline, they would send extra if it was needed.

I think luck was on my side this time. In Kefalonia our neighbours are Suzanne and Owen, they spend all summer out there. Mid March and I had a phone call from Owen, he said he was driving over to Kefalonia early May, and was there anything I wanted taking out, so I asked if he could take some food and a load of other bits and pieces. Owen lives in Swansea so before May we loaded up the car and had an unscheduled visit to Wales. We had a nice time with Suzanne and Owen, staying overnight before the long journey back. Not to mention we had a good time over in Greece which made the waiting more bearable.

When we were in England we used to go over to Todmorden and stay with Derek and Denise for the odd weekend. We were used to the odd accident with my bag coming off, but whilst we were staying at Derek's one weekend we had another surprise in store. On wakening up one morning we found that the bottle that connected to the giving set had leaked all over the bed side cabinet, this was a bit upsetting as the furniture was quite new, and now it had really big stain on it, which wouldn't come out. Derek and Denise were very good about it and said it didn't matter. I offered to pay for it to be repaired but they said no it would be okay.

It was July 2008, and at my HPN clinic appointment Pauline mentioned to the doctor that when she was changing my bag, she had noticed the pipe that went into my fistula was looking a bit suspect. The doctor asked how long had it been in, we told him August 2006, he said that he would get a nurse and fit a new one. Pauline asked if she should go and get a new bag out of the car, he said it wouldn't be a problem he could cut the bag, then stick it back up, so job done and back home.

A couple of days later a nice phone call, surprise, surprise, at that clinic visit my blood test showed that my thyroid level was operable, and so things were set in motion.

Another appointment was arranged for me to see Mr Watson at Wythenshawe Hospital later in the year.

When I saw him they had moved the goal posts so to speak, the muscle was going to be taken out of the top of my leg now, it would be brought up into my abdomen, and the veins left connected, and a skin graft would be taken of the other leg to put on the open tissue. I was told my leg would be left badly scared, like a shark bite he said, but at least I wouldn't have a big hole in my tummy anymore.

Mr Watson was a bit of a joker, he said he didn't think I would be wearing Speedos for swimming anymore.

After I had seen Mr Watson, I received an appointment to go for a CT scan, I presume to see if everything was okay inside my body before the operation was to be arranged. I also had to go for an inspection to determine the length of my rectal stump; this procedure was carried out by Professor Carlson himself. He told me he wanted to know what he was dealing with during my operation. It turned out to be really short, and he didn't hold out much hope of reconnecting my anus, he said he would give it his best shot in the operation.

So waiting patiently for an operation date, everybody kept saying to me you should sue the NHS. I thought nothing ventured nothing gained, and so a solicitor was contacted who did no win no fee, (that's a joke), there is nothing free in this world. He thought I had a very good case, the only problem was the time factor, apparently the case has to be presented before a 3 year period is up, and it's not from the date of the operation, it is from the date you are diagnosed, which in my case was October 2005. I didn't contact my solicitor until late April 2008, so it didn't give us long; I gave him every bit of information possible.

His next move was to get all the medical records, which took a while, and cost X amount, he then got a report on the VACS machine, (vacuum assisted closure system), which looked promising. The NHS had ordered a study on the said machine, for its suitability of use on certain applications, and it had been deemed dangerous in certain applications. Next a court case had to be set up against the NHS, (and paid for). Next an independent specialist on bowel surgery had to be found, who had no connections with the NHS. Mr Duthie a Professor with the right qualifications was found at Hull. So I had to travel over to the other side of the country for an appointment with this Professor, to state my case and all the upheaval it had caused me, he was very thorough and seemed to cover every detail. It seemed like months before his report came through, my solicitor kept pestering his secretary as the time factor was nearing completion. Apparently when a case is registered it is possible to get an extension, we had to do this whilst waiting for his report. More expense!

I can't understand why it took so long as his bill was extortionate.

Eventually my solicitor sent me a copy of the draft, and to put it in a nutshell he said he didn't think the NHS was negligent. In his report the Professor goes through all stages of my time in Lancaster hospital, and apparently all my treatment there was competently carried out, his final opinion reads and I quote:

"Overall then, after the leak, the vac pack is almost certainly partly responsible for his fistula formation. It was however used within its own guidelines as there was tissue between the small bowel and the vac pack at the time of its application. Since the wound was constantly renewing and continuing to granulate that tissue although weak, would have been thickening up. This was in my opinion an unfortunate complication after a very complicated recovery from a leaked anastomosis. I don't think that the team where negligent in any of their management decisions..."

The Barrister's conclusion.

My instructing Solicitor has already commissioned a report from Mr Duthie which summarises the unfortunate history after his initial surgery.

Mr Duthie whose reports I have seen in other clinical negligence cases I have been involved in is very experienced colorectal surgeon and medical legal expert. He has analysed each incident and has concluded that the surgery was competent and in accordance with current practice and guidelines and not negligent. The closest he gets to criticism of the defendants is over the use of the vac pack which he is satisfied materially contributed to the formation of the fistulas. However he exculpates the defendants' staff from blame because the device was not used directly on the bowel and was used within the guidelines for the use of such devices. He regards the development of fistulas as an unfortunate complication after a very complicated recovery from a leaked anastomosis and he considers that the management of the Claimant's case was acceptable.

Accordingly, whilst I would be happy to be corrected by my instructing Solicitor if I have missed something, it seems to me that Mr Duthie's report is not simply not entirely helpful, in my view it provides no basis at all for the Claimant to advance a claim for clinical negligence.

We could seek a second opinion from another colorectal surgeon, but I do not see any point in going to this trouble and expense, because even if the second surgeon was more supportive, it would not get round the problem of overcoming the effect of Bolam v Friern Hospital Management Committee (1957) 1 W.L.R.582. This authority which as stood the test of time, says that a doctor is not guilty of negligence if he has acted in accordance with a practice accepted as proper by a responsible body of medical men skilled in that particular form of treatment; nor is he negligent merely because there is a body of opinion which would adopt a different technique.

So the effect of Bolam is that even if we were able to find a surgeon to support the Claimant's claim, it is certain from Mr Duthie's report that there would be a body of reputable medical opinion that the Defendants could call on which would agree with Mr Duthie's analysis of liability and causation so the claim would fail.

Accordingly I very much regret to advise that I have to advise in my view this claim as no realistic prospect of success.

So we decided to drop the case, as our Solicitor said we could carry on, but the cost could get astronomical and with little hope of winning.

This no (Win no Pay) cost in the excess of £2.000.00 to find out I had no claim.

Well back to the plot. I had an appointment made for a pre op examination for mid October 2008, which I duly attended; at last things were looking favourable as I passed my pre op with flying colours.

The next step and I had to go and see Professor Carlson to discuss the impending operation, as in all visits a follow up letter is sent to me and my GP; I will copy this letter for you.

Date/Time of Appt: 06 November 2008 at 15:10
Clinic: POOLED GEN SURGERY
Type of Appt: Follow_ Up

I am writing to summarise the results of the discussion we had today in my outpatient clinic. You have a huge abdominal wall defect with fistulating loops of small intestine and an end colostomy, following pelvic surgery to resect a cancer undertaken in Lancaster three years ago which led to failure of the join to heal and severe abdominal infection, treated by VAC therapy.

You are currently being fed through "fistuloclysis" with a tube placed in the most distal open piece of bowel.

I have explained that options for dealing with this are limited, but essentially we would plan to resect all the remaining fistulating small bowel and reconstruct the huge abdominal wall defect.

I have explained that, although you have a colostomy in the left side of the abdomen, I cannot guarantee we will be able to reconnect this to the very small piece of rectum which is left behind.

I have explained that, if we do explore your pelvis to see if this is possible, this carries a risk of injury to your pelvic nerves, particularly those involving the bladder and the penis which can lead to permanent or temporary problems with bladder emptying or impotence.

I have explained that this is extremely major complex surgery. I have explained that it carries a risk to your life of the order of 10%. I have explained that we will definitely need an intensive care bed afterwards and it will involve a surgical team including Mr. Stuart Watson, Consultant Plastic Surgeon, at University Hospitals of

South Manchester. I understand he has already discussed with you the technique he proposes to use, namely use of flap from the thigh which will be brought in place to try and fill the abdominal defect.

I have explained that mobilising of the bowel enabling us to remove the piece with holes in may carry the risk of injury to the remaining bowel, which could lead you with temporary or pertinent intestinal failure and a need therefore for temporary or permanent parenteral nutrition.

I have explained that, at the end of surgery, it is likely you will be left with a double barrelled stoma involving the pieces of bowel that currently work through and which you are fed, which we would attempt to close at a latter stage.

I have explained that there are risks involved in bringing up the flap, such that severe infection may prejudice healing of the flap, leading to further hernia formation within the abdomen.

I have explained that surgery carries risks of bleeding, as well as heart problems and problems with blood clots.

I have indicated that the only other option for dealing with your problem would be to resect the holes in your bowel but try and fill the defect in your abdomen with a large piece of absorbable mesh, which would lead almost certainly to a large hernia requiring separate attention, perhaps six months to a year latter, and this is clearly less than ideal.

You have indicated that, having discussed these issues with me on many occasions before, you are happy to proceed and asked me to undertake the surgery for you as soon as I can. I have indicated that, following my discussion last week with Mr Watson, we propose to do this procedure for you in January 2009.

I have written to you so that you have the opportunity to further assess the contents of the letter and determine if there are further questions you need to ask me. You have however, gone round to the Pre Operative Clinic for assessment and been put on my waiting list for this procedure.

GORDEN L CARLSON
CONSULTANT SURGEON
HONORARY PROFESSOR OF SURGERY

Eventually a date was set for the 22nd of January for my operation; all I had to do now was to keep free from infection, as that would be the last thing I needed to be told I couldn't have my op because I had flu or something, after all this time.

Are you ready for the punch line? Early January and I received a phone call from the Professor's secretary, informing me my operation had been cancelled due to unforeseen circumstances. Not very pleased with the news I asked in rather an angry voice when it was likely to be, she said she was very sorry and at the earliest it would be March. I asked why it had been cancelled, she said she couldn't tell me the details, but the date was needed for a life saving operation. After I came off the phone I was so upset, I said to Pauline let's go away somewhere. As it happened we have some friends who live in Southern Ireland near Dublin, and they had been asking us to go out to stay with them for awhile. No further ado, we booked the ferry from Liverpool and had a week's holiday, it was the first time I had been to Ireland and really enjoyed it, I will certainly be going back again sometime.

In February Allison, the Professor's secretary rang to ask me if March the 19th would be okay for me to have the operation. Of course I said yes, she said I would have to have another pre op as the last one would be out of date as they only last 12 weeks. She said she would arrange another and let me know the date.

A few weeks later I had another pre op just a mini one this time, everything okay, all systems go.

March was soon with us, and on Friday the 13th Allison rang. Pauline answered the phone and as soon as she heard Allison's voice she shouted down the phone "not again". She wasn't cancelling the op this time, she was just ringing to see if I could go into Hospital on the Tuesday instead of the Wednesday, as the Professor had to go down to London on the Wednesday. Because it was such a large operation he needed to talk to me before the operation.

I was advised to arrive at Hope Hospital on ward B2 at about lunch time on the Tuesday 17th of March. The procedure is that you ring the ward at 8am on the day of admittance to see if there is a bed available. On ringing there wasn't a bed but was told to arrive between 12 and 12-30pm and if there was still no bed's I would have to wait in the day room until there was a bed available.

CHAPTER TWELVE

Return to Hope

The morning of the 17th arrived and the necessary phone call made. As expected no bed was available, but come anyway. We got to Hope for about 11-30am and decided to go to Stotts Bistro for some lunch before going to the ward. We got to the ward by 12-30pm as instructed and proceeded to make ourselves comfortable in the visitors room until a bed was available. It was a good job we went for some lunch as we sat in that room for about 4hours without as much of an offer of a drink.

While we were sat waiting the Professor came, he was concerned I didn't have a bed; he said he would come back later to explain the op, but whilst he was here he wanted to know if I would give my consent for the use of my good bowel that he was going to cut away, for research. Apparently they test the rate that drugs or medication absorbs in the bowel. He told me that animals used to be used for these tests, but apparently animal gut is different than human gut, so the tests were giving wrong information. So I signed the consent form and he went away happy, a few minutes later he popped his head through the door and told me there would be a bed for me shortly. About ten minutes later I had a bed. After Pauline got me settled in she went off to my daughter's house, she lives not too far from Hope Hospital. She planned to stay there for the duration of my stay in Hospital.

After I had got settled a nurse arrived with a clip board then she proceeded to ask loads of questions. I was then swabbed for MRSA, weighed, and my observations done. She then left. More or less straight away two doctors arrived. One was a trainee, the senior doctor started to ask all the same questions that the nurse had just asked, they were about three quarters way through the questions when the Professor popped his head through the curtain, he asked them to give him 15 minutes. The two doctors then disappeared, never to be seen again. The Professor then started to explain the procedure He told me it was going to be a long operation estimated at 16 hours, his part would take about 12 hours and would involve separating my bowel, which he said was very complex surgery (as it was like separating Siamese twins). He would then site, what he called a back to back jejunostomy on the right hand side of my body. (Actually it is two pieces of bowel, one coming from my stomach, and one coming from my large bowel), these are planned to be joined together later in the year. So back to the plot, he said such a large operation didn't go without the anticipation of problems; there was a chance of severing a nerve which meant I wouldn't be able to get an erection. He said to help reduce this problem he could put stents into my bladder. There was a big chance of heavy bleeding, the chance of too much bowel having to be removed, which would mean having to have assisted food for the rest of my life. Of course the best bit, there was a 10% chance of death in the operation. He told me I would be in intensive care for at least a week, and lots of pipes and tubes coming out of my body. The other part of the operation would be done by Mr Watson and his team of plastic surgeons from Wythenshawe Hospital. This would take approximately 4 hours; this was to rebuild the hole left in my abdomen with the muscle out of my upper leg. It would be cut out with the vein left connected and fastened into the hole, this is called a flap, then a skin graft taken off the other leg and put on the one the muscle had been taken from. I was told that I would have to keep my leg bent at 45 degrees for two weeks. He then asked me if I had any questions. He estimated I would be in Hospital for about 4 weeks, and he said he would get someone to get some blood to see if everything was okay for the op.

After he had left a junior doctor arrived to take my blood, I thought here we go, in my experience doctors are no good at taking blood. He tried for about 10 minutes in three different veins to no avail, so he went away and said he would send a nurse. About 10 minutes later a nurse arrived it took her all of 30 seconds to get 4 tubes full; it just goes to show there is no substitute for experience.

About 5-30 and tea arrived, and not long after another doctor with a lady doctor this time, asking more questions, she needed to know my medication, whoops, the list was in Pauline's hand bag, so I told her it was the same as when I had my pre op. She said she would get it off the computer. The visiting hours on B2 were 3pm till 4pm and 6-30pm till 8pm, so at 6-30 Pauline arrived to spend the next 1 $\frac{1}{2}$ hours with me. She hadn't been with me long and I needed to go to the toilet, as I started to walk to the toilet I felt something wet on my leg, I bet you can't guess? My bag had started to leak; I couldn't believe it as we had put a new bag on on Monday evening, so on my return Pauline pulled the curtains round the bed and on further inspection we found that the bag had come away from the skin at the side, this was strange as it was the first time it had ever come away in this place. As it happened Pauline managed to repair it with some double sided adhesive pads and some opsite, which saved a long job of putting a new bag on. I thought there's no point in putting a new bag on when they will have to take it off for the operation, it took a while to patch me up and by the time we had finished visiting time was nearly over. Pauline remarked that was just what she had wanted to do when she had come to visit.

The evening passed quite quickly, I watched the television in the day room until about 11pm. The rest of the night though was what you might call a nightmare, the guy in the bed opposite was called Stan, I don't think he was very well, as he kept fidgeting; this caused the line in his arm to stop the flow, which in turn made the machine bleep until a nurse came to reset it. I was just dropping off to sleep and BLEEP, BLEEP, BLEEP; this happened about 12 times until someone came and put him a new canula in his arm. Everything went quiet for a while until he started trying to get out of bed, so the nurses had to get him out of his bed and sit him in his chair, he just got settled and he wanted to get back in bed, what a night.

On the Wednesday nothing much happened, a few visits from different people, the pharmacist came to list all my medication, and just after lunch the anaesthetist arrived to talk me through the operation, and precisely what his job would entail.

The room I was in had seven beds; all the guys in there were quite talkative, except for old Stan who was catching up with the sleep he had missed the night before, I am thinking it could be another sleepless night, I am sure he is nocturnal.

Pauline came to visit in the afternoon and we decided to go into the day room, we hadn't been in there long before Mr Slade came to see me. He introduced himself and told me he was going to assist Professor Carlson in the operation, he then proceeded to tell me the same things that the Prof had told me the day before. He also explained in more detail about the plastic surgery, how that all the nerve ends had to be connected, and load's of gorier details, its all clever stuff though. Mr Slade then said he was off home now he was going to get to bed early as it was going to be a long day tomorrow.

Now I thought when you were going to have an operation on your bowel, you had to be nil by mouth for 24 hours, I know I hadn't to have anything to eat or drink before my op in Lancaster, but things must have changed, it was now nothing to eat or drink after midnight the night before your operation.

I asked the Professor about this when he came to see me on Wednesday evening on his way home from London; he actually arrived in visiting hours when Pauline and my daughter Natalie were there, he wasn't best pleased, as the blood test I had on Tuesday hadn't been done properly, so no further ado another blood test, hopefully they would get this one right. Professor Carlson said he was going home now for something to eat, (without wine), and then to bed, he told me to be ready for 7 to 7-30 as he wanted to get an early start.

After visiting I went into the day room to watch telly for a while with a couple of other chaps out of the ward. I turned in about 10-30 as I had to be up early the next day. I actually slept quite well and Stan seemed to keep nice and quiet too. So at 6-15 Thursday morning I got up and went for a shave and shower. When I got back a nurse took my observations, then my feet and legs were measured for my Bobby socks. When they arrived I was pleased to see they were a dark grey colour and not white like the ones I had to wear in Lancaster. I then got into my operating gown and lay on the bed awaiting my fate.

I think it was nearly 8am when Mr Slade arrived, he said the trolley would be here any minute to take me to the theatre, but before I went he wanted to know if I would give my permission for the operation to be videoed, and photographed, as it was such complex surgery, and as the Professor and himself were going to a conference in California later in the year, the footage would help as it was ground breaking surgery, so I agreed and he went away happy saying I will see you shortly.

Well I laid there, 9am came and went, 9-30 came and went, I was beginning to wonder what was happening, it was about 9-55 and the Professor arrived, he had come to tell me that the operation was cancelled, (Apparently there were no available beds on ICU). He said he had even tried to get a bed on ICU at Wythenshawe Hospital where the plastic surgeon was based but to no avail.

The Professor had told me before that as soon as I went into the theatre there would be a bed reserved for me on ICU, as it was such a large operation I would have to be on ICU for at least a week. He also told me if there was an emergency before I entered the operating theatre the bed couldn't be saved. He told me he wouldn't even consider doing the operation without having a bed on ICU.

It could only happen to me, so the upshot was to go back home and come back next Wednesday for the operation next Thursday. So no further ado I rang Pauline to come and get me and take me home.

Two despondent people having to travel back home, I don't think we said more than 10 words each all the way home.

CHAPTER THIRTEEN

The Big Operation

I had been told to be back at Hospital for 12am, on the Wednesday 25th of March, and to be honest everything was exactly the same as it was the week before. I was given a bed about 1-30pm, and to my surprise I was given my own room for my one night stay, it had a television and was on suite. Then all the usual stuff, bloods, obs, etc, I was told I could eat and drink until midnight, and hopefully someone would come for me about 7-30 in the morning.

During the afternoon a different anaesthetist came to see me, I can't remember his name but anyway he explained everything that was going to happen in the operation, from an anaesthetists point of view, and said he would be with me right from the start to the very end no matter how long it took. Early evening and the Professor came to see me, he said things were looking good for the morning, and my blood results were good. So after Pauline had gone I watched telly until about 11pm then turned in.

There was just one thing I wasn't looking forward to and that was the thought of going to ICU for a week, I had such bad memories of my last experience on ICU in Lancaster. The only saving factor was, that I was going on to ICU this time to recover from a operation and not for them to try to save my life.

After a good night sleep which I thought was amazing, I rose about 6-30 am had a shave and a shower, you've got to look your best for an op! Ready for the fray I laid on the bed waiting. About 7-15 and a doctor came in and told me everything was all systems go, and there was a bed on intensive care ready and waiting, he said there was a trolley on its way. At about 7-45 Professor Carlson came into my room and remarked on the fact that nobody had been for me yet, so no further ado he went and got my notes. He told me to put my slippers on and we started to walk to the operating theatre. We had got a fair way up the corridor and there were two guys coming towards us with a trolley, the Professor then asked who they going for, when they said my name he told them in sharp words to get me to the theatre as quickly as possible as I needed to be there for 8am, they didn't waste a moment and had me there in a flash. It is usual for the porters to fill in a form at the ward before they take you to the operating theatre, but in this situation they filled the form in, in the lift. One of the porters asked the other, who was that chap who had told them in no uncertain terms to get me to the theatre as quick as possible? The porter told him it was only Professor Carlson. The other one said he hadn't met him before. The first one said you have not met him in the best situation, as he is one of the most influential people in the Hospital.

I was only in the waiting area two minutes when a nurse came and wheeled me into the anaesthetic room; in there the anaesthetist put the epidural in my back, then he put the heart line into the back of my hand, monitors were connected to me, then the mask went over my mouth and nose, I was told to breath slowly and I didn't know another thing until I was awoken by the anaesthetist at 11-15pm Thursday evening.

Apparently and unbeknown to me, this is in layman's terms what happened in the theatre.

First the Professor and his team had cut away all the old skin around the hole in my abdomen, then all the bowel had to be separated, then the fistulas had to be removed, two new ends had to be made and relocated to my right hand side. When this is completed it is called a double ended jejunostomy. Another thing he was going to try to do was to reconnect my large bowel to my anus, but I had been left with a very short rectal stump, and apparently everything down that bottom end had stuck together, so he tried but couldn't do it. As a result my colostomy had to be removed to a different site on my left side.

As a temporary measure I had a super pubic catheter fitted this goes straight into your bladder just above your penis, (I believe this was put in because I had to have two stents put into my bladder). I had three drain tubes in my body two at the bottom of my flap and one at the top; I also had a gastrostomy tube in just under my rib cage.

After the Professor and his team had finished their long toil, it was the plastic surgeons turn. I believe there were five in Mr Watson's team. There job was to fill the hole that had been left where my abdomen had been. They proceeded to cut a very large piece of muscle from my right leg just above my knee to the top of my thigh, approximately 8inch or 20cm wide, the veins were left connected to the muscle, so it had a better chance of knitting to the other part of my body. The muscle was turned at 180 degrees and was fixed where my abdomen used to be, this meant the bit of leg that was nearest to my knee was now at the top of my tummy. The size of my new tummy was 8inch or 20cm x 11inch or 28cm. After this procedure a skin graft was taken of my left leg and grafted on to what muscle was left on my right leg, so that seems to be about it, all done, it only took 15 hours.

CHAPTER FOURTEEN

Intensive Care Unit

Now the fun starts. I remember the anaesthetist saying wake up Mr Pringle, it's all over now, and everything's fine. Then being slid onto a bed, and being sick, but after that I must have gone straight back to sleep.

It was sometime on the Friday when I came round, only to find I was being taken care of by two young nurses, who wasted no time in getting me washed and changing my bed, then they made me comfortable on my side apparently to stop me from getting bed soars on my bottom. To be honest I felt in a lot better condition than I thought I would have, after being under the anaesthetic for such a long time. At this time I had no idea what had been done to me. I was quite pleased not to have any pain, but I did have a button to press to have a shot of morphine if I did have some pain. I realised there were a few alien pieces about my body, such as tubes and wires.

Before I was taken for the operation I was fitted with the compulsory Bobby socks, but when I awoke on ICU I found I had been fitted with these inflatable socks, they were connected to a machine which inflated and deflated them all the time. I had to wear these until I got back to the ward. The nurse in charge of me had to check the pulse in my big toe about every three hours; (it's a good job Ms Bronder didn't work here or she would have been first in the queue to squeeze my toe). Sometimes they couldn't find a pulse so they had to put a machine on it, this never failed, it must have been very sensitive.

When Pauline came to visit me on Friday afternoon she remarked on how good I looked, she said she thought I would still be fast asleep. Of course she wanted to have a look at my tummy, to be fair I hadn't seen it yet so an investigation was in order. It was quite funny really as my leg was still quite brown from when we had been abroad, and where it had been put was white. Pauline said I looked like a Forever Friends teddy bear, it certainly looked odd. Both my legs were heavily bandaged and I was told it would be a few days before the bandages could come off. Another thing I had to keep my right leg bent at 45 degrees for two weeks.

When the Professor came to see me he remarked on how well I had come through the operation, and he told me everything had gone very well and he was pleased with how everything had turned out.

By the next day or two I'd made a remarkable recovery and everything seemed to go well. By the third day I didn't need any oxygen. It was too good to be true.

On the fourth day I felt really uncomfortable like I wanted to go to for a wee really bad. I told the nurse and he was told to flush my super pubic catheter, which he did and it sorted it out for a while, until later that day, when the pain started again. And it was flushed once again. When the neurologist found out what had been done, he said it hadn't to be flushed out again as it could do some damage.

Well later that day the pain started again, I told the nurse he said he would get a doctor. It was quite a while before the doctor came, and by the time he had arrived the pain had got to a point were it was excruciating. Eventually with tears in my eyes he put a catheter down my penis, the relief was fantastic, the pain was so bad I thought my bladder was going to burst. Apparently this happened because small blood clots had blocked my super pubic catheter, (by the way the catheter the doctor put in is called a refal catheter), I'm getting good with all these names don't you think?.

One thing that amazed me about the ICU here was how different it was up to the ICU at Lancaster. My bed was in a lot larger area, you didn't get the feeling you were in bed with the person next to you. Also for some reason you couldn't hear all the buzzers going off, in fact I didn't feel uncomfortable in here at all.

On the fifth day on ICU the plastic surgeon Mr Watson came to remove the bandages on my right leg to see how it was going on. Pauline was just coming to visit when Mr Watson was entering the ward, he asked her to take him to me. She asked him if she could watch when he took the dressing off; he said he couldn't see why not, as you have done all of his wound management all this time. Mr Watson asked the nurse to go and find some dressings; while he was gone he took off his jacket, and put on his latex gloves. He then said to Pauline could you give me a hand, Pauline immediately thought he wanted her to assist him with bandages. To her relief he said could you roll my shirt sleeves up, I always forget to do this before I put my gloves on. When the male nurse arrived back with the dressings he started to take off my bandages, I didn't know whether I wanted to look or not. so I kept my eyes shut and just had a little peep, to tell the truth it didn't look very nice, Pauline (being a butchers daughter) said it looked like a piece of shin beef. Whilst he was sorting my leg out the nurse in attendance kept asking Pauline if she wanted to sit down, but she declined, as a matter of fact Pauline said it looked like the nurse could have done with a sit down. Mr Watson said he would like the dressing changed daily as it was a bit fluffy at the top were the skin graft hadn't taken, (fluffy apparently means not healing very well). He said the other leg had to stay bandaged for a full two weeks, and no way had the dressing to be removed. The thing was now I had to stay in bed for two weeks with my right leg bent, two weeks in bed, it sounds marvellous doesn't it? Believe me it isn't.

While I was on ICU, Professor Carlson told me I could start to eat again; I can tell you that built me up quite a lot.

Only one more day on ICU, and then I was to be transferred to the surgical High Dependency Unit.

CHAPTER FIFTEEN

High Dependency Unit

So on the Wednesday after lunch I was taken on to HDU, both wards are much the same except on here you don't have as many wires connected to you, and there is one nurse to two beds, and sometimes a trainee. It was okay in there but I found it much noisier, and there was a tremendous amount of coming and going. Patients being brought in from an operation one day and taken out the next, one of the bad things on this ward was that with people coming and going so quick you never got to talk to anyone.

On the Friday one of the plastic surgeons came to check on my leg. This time it wasn't Mr Watson but one of his colleagues. He was called Chris, and the first thing he did was to take off the dressing on my leg. The second thing he did was to take a photo of it.

I was developing a bit of a problem on the flap, (it was at the bottom where the veins had been brought up), the skin around this area was going black, and presumably dying off. Chris and the other doctors on this unit didn't seem too concerned as the rest of the flap was in good order.

Chris told the nurse that was looking after me that the dressing on my leg needed to be changed twice a day, and the staples that had been put in to stretch the skin graft could be removed. It was a trainee nurse that was given the tedious job of removing the staples; it took her about 90 minutes to pluck all the staples out, (there were approximately 120 little staples in my leg).

Now with having to have the dressing changed twice a day, I seemed to have a lot of attention from the nurses as it seemed to take "between", 1 hour, to 1-1/2 hours, every time the dressing had to be changed. Things were looking up in other quarters, as I was beginning to eat quite well again, and felt a lot stronger. There is one thing I don't understand though, when you are on such wards as the ICU or HDU, the nurse that is in charge of you for that day, isn't usually assigned to you the next day. She is looking after someone else, so the new nurse that has been assigned to you hasn't a clue what your needs are, and it's up to you to tell the nurse what the other nurse had done. I know that they have notes to read about your condition, but don't you think it would be better if the nurse that originally was in charge of you would still look after you if she was on duty, as she would know what she was doing. That would seem to be common sense to me, (but common sense doesn't seem to come into it). It was also Friday morning when the Professor came to see me; he likewise wasn't too concerned about the bit of my flap that was dying off. He said he thought a new bit would grow underneath, and to leave well alone, he was more concerned with the block on my neck. This is connected to main veins to which the TPN and the drugs are connected too, the Professor said it looked a bit suspect and told the nurse to keep an eye on it as he didn't want any infection, (too late was the cry), on the Saturday morning the block had to be removed. True to form an infection had set in, so the canola's had to be introduced once again, one for the TPN, and one for the antibiotic to be intravenously fed to get rid of the infection, I thought things were going too well!

It was fairly boring on HDU, as the visiting times were only short, and no one to talk to when the nurses weren't in attendance, I just read and watched all the hustle and bustle on the ward. It didn't take long for my infection to clear up; I think it must have just been caught in the early stages. By the Sunday I was getting fed up with having to keep my leg bent, but I knew I had to stick with it.

Monday morning, the Professor arrived and told me he thought I was well enough to go on to B2, the ward I had been on before my operation. He said I would have less chance of contracting another infection on the ward, as there were all sorts of germs floating about here.

CHAPTER SIXTEEN

Back to Ward B2

So later on that day I was transferred to B2, you can't believe how much quieter it was on this ward, you didn't have the same nurse attention, but the nurses on B2 were absolutely fantastic. There were three in particular that just loved to dress my leg; they were Liz, Kat, and Cassy. these three enjoyed doing the dressing as they said they never get large wounds to attend to on this ward, of course there is always an exception to the rule, and there were a couple of nurses that thought it was a real toil.

I liked on this ward, in the next bed to me was Grant; he had Crone's Disease and had been in Hospital for a good few weeks. He was on here the last time I was on this ward, but I didn't get to know him very well then as I was at the other end of the ward. They were trying to build him up for his operation, which was planned for about 5 weeks hence. Grant was only 27, but he was good fun. In the next bed to him was Robin. Robin was a hairdresser and he also had suffered from Crone's Disease, he had just had his operation, when I saw him I thought I knew his face, later I realised I had watched him pass through HDU the week before. Across from Robin was Cyd, to be honest he was a bit of a pain, but he had good reason though, whilst he had been in Hospital his wife had died, then his daughter had an aneurism and died the day after, poor old fellow. Across from Grant was Phil he was another one recovering from an operation to do with Crone's Disease. And across from myself was Stan, remember him? The bad sleeper, he seemed to be okay now, I think they must have injected him with something. Anyway we had some good crack, and the guys gave me lots of stick about how long the nurses spent behind the curtains with me.

I think it was about the second day on B2 when a guy was wheeled into the ward in another bed, they managed to fit it in okay. I can't remember his name, but I remember he was 65 years old and he was in here because he had fallen out of a tree whilst trimming it. He had broken 10 ribs, his shoulder and his arm in two places, everyone on the ward agreed that he should never have been up a tree at his age.

On the Wednesday Chris the plastic surgeon came to see me and altered the regime slightly, from twice to once a day for the dressing. He looked at my flap and said he agreed with the Professor to leave it alone. The next thing he did was to remove the dressing off my left leg and then he took a photo. I had been told it would hurt like mad when the dressing was taken off; I was quietly surprised when it didn't hurt at all, and it just came of like a sheet of brown paper. There were quite a few scabby bits, but I was told to rub it liberally with E45 cream, the part that wasn't scabby looked really good, and my other leg wasn't looking too bad either.

Chris told me I could straighten my leg tomorrow, and probably be able to get out of bed, I couldn't wait.

It all happened on that Wednesday; I went for a contrast x-ray to see if it would be possible to put a pipe down into my large bowel, so I could be fed by the same system I had been on before my operation. The idea was to put me back on distal feed until my next operation, which would be to connect the two ends of my jejunostomy together, which hopefully will give me a continuous bowel, which touch wood would mean no more assisted food or pills etc.

I didn't actually get out of bed for another day or two, something to do with a shortage of Physiotherapist's I was told.

Next day and Pauline was there at afternoon visiting, and I had an unexpected visitor, Steve a good friend who lives on the outskirts of Manchester. He said he was just passing so he just popped in for ½ an hour, I bet he hadn't been there 5 minutes and a porter arrived, they needed me down at x-ray urgently. It turned out they were having a meeting about my contrast study, that had been done the day before, and there was a bit of a problem so I had to be x-rayed at different angles. Of course my visitor had gone by the time I had got back, a bit inconsiderate at visiting, don't you think?

As it happened, everything turned out okay, apparently on the first x-ray my hip bone was in the way, and it was causing concern that something was obstructing the bowel, so later that day a pipe was inserted down my jejunostomy into my large bowel, ready to start the feeding regime again that evening.

Now the only thing was that Kirstein my dietician, had stopped all my previous medication, and my perative feed, this turned out to be a problem quite a while later, which we will cover later in the story.

So back to the feeding thing, I had 1 1/2 ltr of perative, 1ltr of sterile water, mixed with 10 sachets of dioralyte powder fed down the tube into my large bowel, over a period of 12 hours.

The other medication she had prescribed for me was 5 Lopramide tablets 4 times a day, 3 Omeprazole tablets twice a day, and 6 tablets a day for my thyroid problem. I was also eating quite normally now, but unbeknown to me, I didn't get very many nutrients out of the food I was eating.

In my notes were a couple of diagrams, explaining and showing where all the pipes, drains, and wounds were, and instructions on how to attend to them. There is a copy of the diagram at the back of the book.

It was getting close to Good Friday, and everything seemed to be going fine, except for just one small problem which was, every time the dressings was changed on my wounds, about 10 minutes later I was violently ill. It wasn't that I was bothered about looking at the wound, or that it hurt when the dressing was being changed, so I guess it must have been in my subconscious, so the solution was to have an anti sickness injection before I had my dressings changed, it seemed to do the trick.

So Good Friday arrived and 4 out of 6 beds emptied, Grant, Robin, and Phil, went home for a long weekend, to return on the Tuesday, and old Stan was taken off to a nursing home somewhere, so for the Easter weekend it just left Cyd, and myself, to be honest he was as much fun as having diphtheria.

Not to worry as today I was going to take my first steps for a fortnight,. I had to wait for quite a long time before the physiotherapist's arrived, eventually they got me out of bed, and with the aid of a Zimmer frame I managed to take about 6 steps. It seemed quite awkward with all the pipes and things that were attached, but we seemed to manage.

The other thing I was a bit upset about was the size of my belly, with being laid on my back for all this time my belly seemed quite flat, but when I stood up it was quite apparent it wasn't. In my own mind I thought that when the plastic surgeon put the muscle from my leg into my belly, I would have a flat belly, I was wrong, instead of a six pack I was left with a barrel.

On the Saturday I managed to walk a good few more steps, with the aid of the nurses, and the Zimmer frame. The nurses had to do it as it was the Easter Holiday and the physiotherapist's were in short supply. We did well except the wound on my flap bust open, there was blood everywhere, all over the floor, and all over the chair they sat me on, what a mess. After the nurse had sorted the problem out, later that day I attempted another journey that proved successful, well I say that, but with only having only half a muscle in the top half of my leg, so to speak, it kept letting me down, and it was quite painful. I suppose this was something I would have to get used too for a while.

As it was Easter weekend, I was well endowed with a multitude of visitors; also Pauline took me on a push about in a wheelchair all around the Hospital, it felt great to get out of the ward for a while. I couldn't believe how quiet it was around the Hospital, you usually couldn't move in the place. It was Professor Carlson's weekend to be on call, so I was quite pleased to see him every day, he seemed to be very pleased with my progress, and casually asked a nurse to remove one of my many tubes, which coincidently was starting to get very irritating, and quite sore. He told her to remove my refal catheter as well.

He said if things were to keep going as well as they were I could have my super pubic catheter removed in a day or two.

After the professor had been to see me on Monday morning I felt really good, so I asked Kat my nurse if I could go and have a shower, she said I could as long as I was very careful, so she removed my dressing, and I must add my leg looked to be healing really well.

So off I go to the shower with my drip stand and Zimmer frame, I still had some drain tubes connected, and I was still connected to my feeding tube, as I was still being fed through it. My feeding regime had been altered too, 2 litres' of sterile water with 20 sachets of dioralyte over 16 hours.

Anyway I managed to shower my top half, no bother; now common sense sometimes goes out the window. There was a chair in the shower, and why I didn't sit on it to shower my leg I don't know, instead I lifted my good leg up on to the chair, "you've got it", my bad leg gave way, and I ended up on my back in the middle of the shower room. Not only that, but the giving set joint, where it connects is quite bulky, of course sods law, it gouged a great big groove in all that lovely new skin on my leg, there was blood everywhere. Now the emergency pull cord was over the other side of the shower room, it took me ages to slide myself over to it, but eventually I got there and assistance soon arrived. It was Kat that came to my assistance, I was covered in blood with trying to get to the cord, and she said if I had cut my throat I couldn't have looked any worse. A doctor was sent for, he said it was a deep cut but it would heel, so my nice new leg had to be bandaged up again, don't you do stupid things when you're feeling a bit better?

When the Professor had been to see me this morning, (before I had my shower), he told me if I kept making such good progress I could make plans to go home on Friday, (after my accident in the shower today I thought that's upset the apple cart, it's forced to extend my stay in hospital).

On the Tuesday when he visited me, he didn't seem too bothered about my accident, he said that the district nurses would be capable of seeing to all my wounds, so he instructed the nurse to take the last of the tubes out of my body. One of which was my gastronomy tube, which I might tell you was quite painful when it was removed, the tube seemed to have attached itself to my body, which caused me to spike a temperature, and then ended up with a water infection. I thought here we go again, no chance of getting home on Friday now, anyway another canula was inserted and some more antibiotics put to work.

So another day passes much the same as any other, I was still having my leg and that nasty bit at the bottom of my flap dressed everyday. The best thing was my temperature seems to be coming down, which is good.

Thursday morning when the professor came to see me, he said he wouldn't see me tomorrow has he had to go to London, but if my temp was normal in the morning I could go home. I asked him when the stents would be taken out of my bladder, he told me that it would be a few weeks before that would happen, but looking at things realistically; I had done really well to be going home just 3 weeks after such a large operation.

So Friday morning my water works seemed better, and my temp was right, so home James! Things took a bit of sorting out, all my drugs, dressings, release notes, etc, it was mid afternoon by the time we got away. I don't think I was as well as I thought I was, I was absolutely washed out by the time I arrived home, it took us about 1-3/4 hours to get home, Friday traffic you know what its like, anyway at least I was in the comfort of my own home.

CHAPTER SEVENTEEN

Back Home

It was Friday the 17th of April, and I was so pleased to be home, I was so tired I went straight to bed for 3 hours.

Next day we had a houseful, Natalie our youngest daughter, and her husband Michael, with our granddaughter Orla, our oldest daughter Michala, her husband David, with our other two grandchildren Joe, and Maddie. It was so nice to have them here, but you forget how boisterous they can be when they all get together. I managed the mayhem for awhile, and then had to give in and go to bed out of the way. It's amazing how unsociable you can be when you are not very well.

The district nurse was calling to see me twice a day, in the morning to dress my leg, and the bottom of my flap, which seemed to be getting a lot bigger, and messier, and in the evening to attend to the flap.

When I was discharged from hospital I was given a large folder for the district nurses, this was a wound care plan. It contained a diagram similar to the one that was used on the ward to point out the area to be treated, and the method to be used. There were also pictures of the infected area; I suppose the nurses could tell by comparing the picture of my wounds to the actual thing if it was getting any better. In the wound care plan there were a lot of instructions and a lot of report forms to fill in.

There is a care plan at the end of the book for the parts of my leg and my flap that needed attention by the district nurses.

This wound on the flap was becoming to be a bit of a pain, as it was constantly weeping, and we couldn't keep the area around it dry. There was also another problem, the wound at the top of my leg was very close to the wound on my flap, and I had been told at hospital that there had to be no cross contamination between the two wounds. That was a joke, as every time my dressings were changed the bandages at the top of my leg were wet through, and in 9 cases out of 10, Pauline had to patch it up to stop it leaking after the district nurses had gone. No disrespect to the nurses, but they didn't seem to take enough time making sure the dressings were stuck down well enough.

Another thing about the district nurses, more than often two nurses arrived to attend to me, and it wasn't unusual for one of the nurses to stand looking out of the window, at the view across the bay to the Lake District. One nurse commented one day that she liked coming to see me as she couldn't believe the view.

On the following Wednesday 22nd of April, I had an appointment at Wythenshawe Hospital to see the plastic surgeon that did all the work on my leg and abdomen. My appointment was for 10-30am, which was a pain as having to get from Morecambe to Manchester early morning is nigh impossible, especially were the M61 joins the M60 it's a nightmare. A 1 hour journey takes 2 hour's at that time of day. With it only been just over 3 week's since my operation, by the time I got to the hospital I was feeling shattered. We had set off from home about 7-45am it was now about 10am when Pauline had parked the car she went and found a wheel chair, and got me to my appointment on time.

At this particular area there are a lot of different departments, such as burns, etc, so you have to book in then take a seat with a few hundred other people. Eventually a nurse comes and calls your name along with about ten others, you then follow this nurse like sheep into a corridor, where there are the most stupid little seats you have ever seen in you life, all down the side of the corridor, these uncomfortable plastic seats fold up to the wall. There must have be 30 to 40 seats, which are all full and most of them are waiting to see the man I am here to see. We had been sat on these most stupid little seats for about 1 hour, and I had the feeling I was going to pass out. So Pauline went and told a nurse about my situation, the nurse in question must have then had a word with Mr Watson the plastic surgeon, he told her to find me a room where I could lie down until he could see me.

When eventually he arrived, he said he thought I was still in Hope Hospital, and he was going to come and see me there tomorrow on Thursday. He said they were doing another operation like mine, unbeknown to me at the time the operation was to be on Denise Hendry, the footballers wife, you have probably heard about it, she had complications after the same operation as I had had, and died.

Anyway he wanted to cut open the bottom of the flap, to get rid of all the infection in there, he also thought it would be a good idea to put a skin graft on the top part of my leg, the bit where the skin graft hadn't taken in the first place.

Then he sent for someone to take a load of photographs of my leg, and my flap. This is something I couldn't get my head round, how many photos do they need? They must have taken at least 100 since my first visit to see him.

At the end of my appointment he said we had to make another appointment to see him in two weeks, he said he would get in touch with Professor Carlson, to have a discussion with him about what he thought was the best thing to do.

A nurse found me some special cream, she said I wouldn't be able to get anywhere else, which would work wonders on my leg.

On arriving home there was an appointment from Hope to see the skin viability nurse on, Thursday 7th of April, the day after my next appointment at Wythenshawe, so Pauline rang Hope and explained about the appointment at Wythenshawe. After a while they rang back from Hope, and told us they would cancel the Wythenshawe appointment and just come to Hope on the Thursday as arranged.

For the next two weeks everything seemed to be going well, except in myself I was feeling a bit weak and not really very well, but my leg on the other hand was healing quite well; it must have been that special cream I had been given. I was walking a bit better now, and my muscle seemed to be getting stronger.

The only down side was this wound under the flap, all this pus kept running out, it didn't bother anybody else but the constant smell that came out of it made me feel sick all the time.

It was bank holiday weekend, and our friends Derek and Denise came over on the Sunday for lunch, it was about 2pm and Pauline was just about to serve the soup. I said I would just go to the toilet before lunch, to my surprise when I was in the toilet I found that the front of my underpants were wet through with this pus stuff, so I told Pauline to hold lunch for a little while, as I thought my dressing had come loose, and we had better go and fix it.

After further investigation we found that a hole had appeared, I thought it was coming from where the super pubic catheter had been, but it turned out later it was where one of the stitches on the bottom of the flap had been.

So Pauline patched me up, and I enjoyed the rest of the day.

It was Bank Holiday Monday the next day, and when the district nurse came to attend to my dressings she was concerned, and sent for the emergency doctor.

The night before there was quite a lot of pus coming out, so Pauline put a small stoma bag over it to catch the pus, so I would be dry overnight

When the emergency doctor arrived she put me on antibiotics, I told her I had an appointment on Thursday at Hope to see the skin viability nurse, and the dietician.

So on Thursday at Hope, I told the dietician I wasn't feeling to be getting any better, and asked her if she could check my bloods, to see if I was getting enough nutrients. I also told her I was losing weight, she told me to start having an extra 500 ml of perative, distally fed into my large bowel nightly.

The reason I wasn't feeling too good was that Kirsten the dietician hadn't put me on enough supplements, I think somewhere along the line she hadn't understood what I had had done. When I mentioned it to Professor Carlson he said I should have been on the same amount of nutrients as I had had before my operation, as nothing had changed as my bowel was not continuous. So after a few weeks it all got sorted out and it didn't take long before I was feeling good again.

The skin nurse was pleased with the progress of my leg, but she was puzzled with the pus coming out of this hole, so she contacted the Professor to come and have a look. He said he couldn't get down to see me today but he wasn't too concerned, and to take a swab of the pus coming out of the hole, and from under the flap, which she did, then I had my blood test done and came home.

On Friday, late afternoon we received a phone call from Hope, telling me I had to go to Lancaster A and E urgently for an emergency magnesium infusion. I was told it was all set up, so off we go Friday teatime. Traffic was a nightmare at that time on a Friday. When we got there I had to have a blood test before they would start the infusion. This infusion was going to take 1 hour when it happened. So this male nurse took me into a small office to put a canula into my arm. Pauline and I sat down then the nurse sat on a office chair with wheels, he picked up the items needed and pushed himself in the chair at a remarkable speed straight towards me, Pauline stuck her hand out to stop him, then went mad at him saying be careful then proceeded to tell him why. He managed to put a canular into my vein, after the 4th attempt and my blood was taken. Pauline and I went back into the waiting room, after about 1 hour Pauline went to find someone to tell them that it wasn't doing me any good being sat on these uncomfortable chairs all this time, and could they find me a *cubicle* with a bed. They actually then found a room for me, I think it must have been a child's treatment room as all the walls were decorated with jungle book characters. It was a good job I had something too lie on as it was another 2 hours before they started my infusion.

It was a young doctor that came to start the infusion, he couldn't believe what I had been through and the bad luck I had had. I don't think Pauline was in a right good mood as she was very stern with him, and proceeded to tell him that if it hadn't been for Lancaster Infirmary none of this would have happened.

It had only taken 5 hours from start to finish, not bad for a 1 hour infusion, but that's Lancaster Hospital for you.

My next appointment at Hope was on Thursday 14th of May, to see the skin nurse again, still plenty of pus coming out of the hole and under the flap, but otherwise pleased with my leg, another blood test and home again.

On the following Tuesday, I had another phone call from Hope telling me that a prescription had been sent to my doctors, for some antibiotics. I was told not to drink alcohol with these drugs, as they were very strong.

I was getting worried now as my tummy was starting to swell to an enormous size.

My next appointment at Hope was on the 21st of May, and I had been told there had been a card set up for me to have a CT scan on that date. This was to see where the pus was coming from, and going to.

Well on the day of my appointment, the Professor was supposed to be coming to see me, but that day he was the surgeon on call, just my luck, as it happened he was in theatre all the time I was at the Hospital. So consequently because I never saw the Professor, I never got my CT scan, so they took my bloods again, and sent me home.

Friday morning another phone call from Hope, my magnesium was seriously low, same as last time I should go to Lancaster for another infusion. The lady on the phone said she would ring back when it was arranged. About one hour later she rang, telling me they thought it would be better if I came back to Hope for this infusion.

She said I had to bring my overnight things, as they were going to try and sort out my other problem while I was there; it was like being on a yo-yo, back and forth from Morecambe to Manchester.

So Friday 22nd of May, I arrived at Hope at about 2-30 pm, and reported to ward B2, from there I was sent to the assessment ward, where I was told I was expected.

When I arrived there nobody knew anything about me, they said nobody had told them about my arrival, so we had hang about for a while until the cock-up had been sorted out.

Now the assessment ward is something else. Really I shouldn't have ever been sent to this ward, the amount of times I had been in this Hospital I should have gone straight on to B2.

Well now I am here, I am subjected to every sort of test possible, a form like war and peace to fill in, a swab taken in every orifice, a blood test, an X-ray, urine sample, and my observation's taken, all this for a magnesium infusion, what a waste of N H S money.

About 4-30 I asked if I could have something to eat, I was told no as I was nil by mouth until the doctor had seen me in case I needed on operation. I think someone had got their wires crossed somewhere, I will tell you I was ready for walking out of that place.

About 5-30pm a junior doctor arrived he asked me about a 1,000 questions, he said it was okay for me to eat, and proceeded to tell me that he was only the registrar, and the doctor would be round shortly, so shortly after a nurse arrived with a sandwich and a cup of tea.

It was about 6-30pm when a doctor, I knew from when I was in Hospital before, popped his head round the curtain, and said I have something to attend to, but I will be with you shortly.

At about 8-30pm, Pauline decided to go home, this was because a nurse had just been to see me, and told me that the doctor had been called to do a small operation, and that I would have to have a magnesium infusion overnight.

It was about 9-30pm when the doctor eventually arrived, I told him I needed to go on to my distal feed shortly, he said I would have to go on to another ward for that, and any other treatment I needed, as this was just an assessment ward. He then told me I was going on to B2 when a porter was available. I told him I could walk round to the ward; he said it wasn't allowed, health and safety.

Now from 9-30 to 10-30, I never saw a soul, I think it was because earlier on in the evening there had been a dispute between the two nurses, and the matron, and I think they had taken the huff, and disappeared off somewhere in protest. Eventually a nurse appeared, and I asked how much longer I had to wait, she said a porter was on his way, at 10-55pm the porter arrived with a wheel chair, I sat in the wheel chair and he pushed me 150 yards to ward B2, how stupid! I could have been there 1-1/2 hours earlier, if they had let me walk.

As it happened I knew the nurses well on this ward. Chris was in charge this evening, I asked him if he could sort out my distal feed, which he did quite quickly. He said he had sent for the nurse to come and put a canula in my arm, so that I could have the infusion.

The next three days were bordering on the worst I had ever spent in hospital; how a ward can change from the last time I was there.

First the chap in the next bed never stopped coughing, the chap straight across from me, slept all day, and shouted out all night, and the chap on the other side of me was overdosing on drugs, he was hallucinating, and screaming a load of nonsense all night. The only person on the ward with any personality was Stuart; he was in the bed at the far end of the ward. Just my luck the only person I could talk to that made any sense went home Saturday.

It was Friday night / Saturday morning, about 1-30am when the nurse came and put a canula in my arm. About 1 hour later another arrived nurse with a drip stand and machine, she connected me to the first part of my infusion, and told me it would take about 1 hour, and then the next part would take 24 hours. True to form the alarm on my machine started beeping at 3-15, to denote the finish of the dose. I was disconnected and about 4 am I was connected for my 24 hour dose, if the other patients hadn't kept me awake, I don't think I would have slept much with all the activity round my bed.

8-30am and needing match sticks to keep my eyes open, the ward doctor and his entourage arrived, he had a look at the site where the pus was coming out, and he agreed that I needed a CT scan to see what was happening under the flap. On further discussion the doctor decided to leave the CT scan until a weekday, due to staffing levels at the weekend, and it wasn't causing me to have a temperature, nor was I feeling ill, so it wasn't deemed important.

Back to the happy ward! There was only one guy that spoke to me, and he went home on Saturday morning, so all day Saturday I just sat reading until visiting at 3pm. I couldn't go very far as I was connected to my magnesium infusion.

Saturday night was just as bad as the Friday night, constant coughing, and shouting, all night long.

The chap across from me, his bed was under the window. It was in the middle of the night when he got out of bed and started trying to get out of the window, so I pressed the nurse call, the nurses came running and got him back in bed.

It was 4am Sunday my infusion finished, so in the morning when the day shift started, I asked Angelo the male nurse in charge, (as nothing was going to be done to me today), could I go out for the day if Pauline came and picked me up. He said I could go after my blood had been checked if it was okay. Now you know how fast hospitals work, it was about 10-30am when the nurse arrived to take my blood, and the result didn't come back until 3pm. It's now visiting time again, and too late to go anywhere, so another miserable day in hospital sat amusing myself.

Monday morning, after what had seemed to be an endless night Professor Carlson arrived on his ward round. After a close inspection he said I needed a CT scan, he was worried that the pus was going into my bladder. Now with him in charge, I thought it will happen this morning or at least this afternoon, how wrong you can be! Monday lunch time I was informed that my CT scan wasn't going to happen until late Wednesday afternoon, talk about being devastated. And to cap it all, the guy in the next bed that was hallucinating was moved, and a young guy came into his bed, I said hello to him, and he turned his back on me, drawing his curtain between us. When Pauline came to visit at 3pm I told her I had to get out of this place before I went crazy.

So after a lot of discussion with the nurses, a doctor was sent for. He didn't seem too keen to let me go home, but after he had spent a considerable time on the phone he let me go home, on the condition that I took a course of this solution at prescribed times, this was for the CT scan, and that I would return back to Hope on Wednesday afternoon.

I seem to remember it was about 6pm we eventually got out of that place, I will tell you something, it's a lot easier to get into hospital, than it is to get out, it makes you think it would be easier to get out of Colditz.

On the Wednesday afternoon on arriving at ward B2, I was told I had been moved on to B4, this is the intestile failure unit, the ward I was on for 4 months the first time around.

On arriving at the ward, I was surprised to see Stuart; he was the only guy on B2 that spoke to me, before he went home on the Saturday morning.

On the ward Stuart was in the next bed to me, he lived in Sunderland, and across from him was Chris, he came from near Bath.

The young lad in the bed next to Chris was a bit of an oddity, he never spoke to anyone. He used to go home every day, and come back in the evening to be connected to his TPN. He would then disappear into the day room, and come to bed at some unearthly hour, and then it would take the nurses all morning to get him up. After he had been disconnected from his TPN, his mum came and he went home again.

On the other side of Stuart was Paul, he was very sick man, he looked like what I must have looked like, when I was in intensive care, poor fellow.

The crazy thing is, Stuart, Chris, and I had had our fistula problem caused by that controversial VACS machine, apparently they had also tried to claim, but to no avail.

It makes you wonder though, how many people have had the same problem with this machine and not made it to Hope, or even died in the process.

Back to the CT scan, it was arranged for 4-50pm, and all went according to plan, of course I had to be taken there and brought back in a wheel chair, I suppose it finds someone a job.

Next day after the results had been studied; I was told that it was just a cavity that had formed between where the flap had been joined to what was left of my abdomen.

The next problem was, they couldn't tell if any of the fluid was going into the bladder, or if it was going anywhere else.

The next test would involve having some dye put into one of these holes, and x-rayed, to see where it was tracking to.

I was told this wouldn't happen until next week, and as I seemed well and didn't have a temperature, I could go home for the weekend. As it happened it was Bank holiday weekend, so I didn't have to go back until Tuesday morning.

Back at hospital on Tuesday, and early afternoon a doctor arrived with a kidney bowl full of stuff, no further ado, he stuck a pipe down one of the holes. He then connected the pipe to a syringe full of water, and started to flush the cavity out, all this stuff, and then the water came out of the other hole, he said that was good, then he left.

Nothing happened on Wednesday and it didn't seem as if anything was going to happen on Thursday neither, the only thing that was certain was, I had an appointment with the skin viability nurse on Thursday afternoon.

I think it was Wednesday afternoon when Fred arrived; the nurses moved things around a bit to make room for another bed in the ward. So Fred took occupancy of his bed, he must have only been in his bed about five minutes when he broke wind very loudly. I think this was something to do with his bowel problem as he never stopped breaking wind. This caused a lot of frivolity down at our end of the ward and it didn't take long to nickname him Farty Fred. On the ward we had a male black nurse who had a fantastic sense of humour, I can't remember his name but one day I asked him if he had a wine cork, he asked what I wanted with a cork, I said if you get one can you stick it up Fred's bum, he started to laugh that much I thought he was going to split his sides.   Thursday afternoon and I was in with the skin viability nurse for her to check on my legs, and my flap where it was a mess, when she noticed on the left hand side of my tummy, where the stitches were, it looked puffy and red, so she poked it, and a load of pus came out of these stitches. I don't know but I think when the doctor pumped all that water in, it must have moved the infection further on where the flap had been joined.

So that the pus could flow out uninterrupted, another small bag was stuck over the hole, (now I had three bags stuck on the bottom of my tummy), with the other two stoma bags one at each side that was five altogether, I didn't half look a sight, I felt like a Christmas tree.

So Friday arrived and still no sign of a contrast study, so once again I was told to go home for the weekend and come back on Monday, and the contrast study would happen next week.

Another nice weekend at home, and the weather was fantastic for a change. Back to the Hospital on Monday and on arrival I was told to stay on the ward as my bloods needed taking, and also the doctor wanted to see me.

Now on B4 the visiting times were relaxed, with no set times, so Pauline spent most of Monday with me.

I think it was about 2pm when the blood nurse arrived to relieve me of a few tubes of blood, and it was 4-30pm when the doctor came to see me, and all she wanted was to see if I had been okay over the weekend. She also told me my contrast study would be on Thursday morning at 9am.

So Tuesday morning I asked if I was needed for anything, I was told that nothing concerning me was happening, so I asked if I could go to my daughters for the day. I was told that it would be okay, so no further ado, I rang Pauline to come and pick me up about 10am, and had a lovely day in the back garden at Natalie's house in Manchester.

Wednesday I had an appointment to see the plastic surgeon at Wythenshawe Hospital.

This Hospital is at the other end of Manchester about 45 minutes away.

True to form my appointment was for 11-30 in the morning. I actually saw Mr Watson at 1-30pm, and that was a waste of time. He said he thought that it would be better to cut open under the flap, clean it out and fasten it back together, so he gave me a letter to give to Professor Carlson relaying his thoughts.

After we left Wythenshawe we didn't go straight back to Hope, we went to the Trafford Centre and had a lovely Chinese meal before returning.

Thursday morning up for my appointment at 9am, and ready for the contrast study. I had been to this department that many times I was regarded as a regular. I was all done and back on the ward by 9-45am.

I knew the result before the doctor arrived to tell me, as I had watched it on the screen down at the ex-ray unit, and the radiographer pointed out that the pus showed up in black lines, and it wasn't tracking anywhere it was just laying in the cavity it had made.

So eventually when the doctor came to tell me the good news, he said when the Professor had seen the results I would probably be able to go home.

So Thursday tea time I was kicked out so to speak, not for long though.

Monday morning and back to Hope again, this time to have the stents removed from my bladder. This was an unknown entity, and I wasn't looking forward to it. I had been told they were extracted through your penis.

So there we were Monday looking for the urology unit, on finding it I wasn't sat waiting long before a rather large nurse came and took me into a room to get changed. I thought that they might have nurses this large to sit on you in case you started to struggle, well anyway she gave me a surgical gown and told me to get undressed and to put the gown on, she said she would come to collect me shortly.

About 10 minutes later she came for me and took me down a corridor to another room, which had a narrow bed, a television screen, and a trolley with some syringes and the thing that concerned me most, was a very long thin tube with what looked like a light bulb at the end, and at the other end it was like a gun handle with controls on it, I looked at this thing and broke out into a sweat.

I was told to lie on my back on the bed, and pull my gown up above my waist. A doctor and another chap arrived, he said not to worry it wont take long, I thought it's all right for you mate your not lying here.

So he picked up a syringe and stuck down the end of my penis, he said it was gel with a slight anaesthetic, after a minute or two he picked up this terrifying thing off the trolley and started to insert down my penis, the first push made my eyes water, but after that it wasn't too uncomfortable.

So the search started for these illusive stents, it took a while to find the first one, and when found a claw came out of this camera come light thing that was in my bladder, it took a bit of a struggle to get hold of it, then it was pulled out not just straight but double at one end, that made my eyes water even more than when the camera went in.

I bet you are wondering how I know all this; well I watched it all on the television screen next to my bed.

Ready for round two, the same thing over again only this time they couldn't find the next stent as everything in my bladder was cloudy. The doctor asked me if I had emptied my bladder before the operation, I said I had, he said there was a lot of urine in there and it would have to come out.

So out came the camera, and in goes a catheter to drain all the excess urine out before he could resume is search.

Round three, when the camera had been inserted the search continued but he couldn't find the next stent, he seemed to be looking for a long time, then he said to me did you have more than one stent in. I said I didn't really know but surely if it had only been one, it would have said stent and not stents in the letter.

So then the doctor sent a nurse to look in my notes to find out if it was one or two.

After a few minutes she came back with the answer, it was two, so here we go again, this time after about 10 minutes of searching he caught a glimpse of it, the doctor commented on how far it had gone up into my bladder, so eventually it was extracted to my relief. So walking like John Wayne red eyed and quite sore downstairs I was told I could go home.

On my way back to the car I said to Pauline I feel like I want the toilet, so at the Hospital entrance I went to the toilet, to my surprise when I started to have a wee and it sprayed everywhere, it was just like a shower head. I thought they could have warned me about that, so back home, and I can tell you I was quite sore for a day or two.

Here we go again, Thursday morning and back on the road down to Hope, this time to see Professor Carlson, I think my appointment was for 2-50pm, I don't think I had to wait too long after my allotted time, when he saw me he told me that he wasn't going to cut under the flap as Mr

Watson had suggested. He thought it was too dangerous as he didn't know how near my bowel was to the new flap.

He said it would heal on its own from the middle outwards given time, he said he was pleased that the pus wasn't tracking anywhere.

So the next thing to do he said was, to reverse the double barrelled jejunostomy, he said he hoped to get it done before Christmas, then my bowel should be back to working normal, fingers crossed then.

He said he didn't need to see me again until the end of October, or early November, and when my tummy had healed up I could go out to Kefalonia if I wanted to.

My next clinic appointment was set for the 7th of August so no further ado, Pauline booked a flight out for the 7th of July for two weeks, just what I needed; two weeks in the sun after all I had been through this year.

After I had been home a few weeks a copy letter came, these letters were sent to Dr Sykes my GP.

Professor Carlton sent one out every time I had been to see him, this one was about my operation, I will copy this letter it may explain in more technical terms than I have put it in the book.

Date of Admission: 25 March 2009
Date of Discharge: 17 April 2009

Diagnosis: Intestinal failure, massive abdominal defect with multiple enteroatmospheric fistulae, end colostomy.
Procedure: Laparotomy, resection of multiple enterocutaneous small bowel fistulae, attempted reconstruction of colorectal anastomosis, insertion of bilateral ureteric stents, creation of double-barrelled

ileostomy, plastic surgical reconstruction of abdominal wall with tensor fascia flap.

Paul was admitted for surgery as outlined above. Having endured a considerable period of time with a huge abdominal wall defect, multiple exposed loops of small bowel, and distal feeding, he came in for reconstructive surgery.

On his original admission a couple of weeks earlier, we had to cancel the operation because of lack of availability of an intensive care bed, but happily on this occasion, we were able to proceed.

We were able to gain access to the abdomen with difficulty and eventually undertook a full adhesiolysis, leaving him with 210cm and 180cm of small bowel proximal and distal to a double barrelled stoma.

Unfortunately, it proved impossible to restore colonic continuity. The original dissection had actually been quite low in the pelvis and the rectal stump was stuck like concrete to the bladder base which was inadvertently perforated in trying to mobilise it.

Mr Shackley therefore kindly joined us while we opened and repaired the bladder, inserting bilateral ureteric stents and a supra pubic catheter.

Having abandoned the colonic reconstruction, we simply therefore refashioned the end colostomy to a site on Mr Pringles abdominal wall that we felt he would be able to manage satisfactorily.

Mr Watson and his colleagues then undertook a right tensor fascia lata flap. Finally, we sited a double barrelled ileostomy in the native abdominal wall on his right side, following which Mr Pringle was transferred to the Intensive Care Unit.

Total operating time was in the region of 15 hours. Mr Pringle actually made a remarkable post operative recovery. The only significant problems we had were with an area of flap necrosis in the proximal part of the flap where it joined the abdominal wall on the right hand side, and the urinary tract infection, the latter presenting as a bout of fever shortly after we removed the urinary catheters a few days before Mr Pringle went home.

At the time of discharge from hospital, we had resumed infusion of fluids into the distal bowel as we knew that had kept Mr Pringle stable throughout his pre-operative course at home. I have copied Mr Shackley into this letter so that he can make arrangements to see Mr Pringle with a view to removing the ureteric stents at flexible cystoscopy in the near future.

Ultimately, our plan is to leave Mr Pringle perhaps four to six months longer, and when he is fully recovered from his abdominal reconstructive surgery, undertake a further contrast study down the distal limb of small bowel prior to closing the stoma for him, and leaving him simply with an end colostomy.

I have arranged to see Mr Pringle in my clinic in six weeks time, but he will continue to have follow up in the HPN Clinic.

That ends the letter sent to Dr Sykes, from Professor Carlson.

CHAPTER EIGHTEEN

Life with a megostomy

The trip to Kefalonia once again wasn't the easiest thing in the world; I was still not very mobile so I had to have wheelchair assistance at both airports.

The other problem was, all my medical aids plus the entire luggage, I don't know how Pauline managed to deal with all the stuff, plus me in a wheelchair, but she did and we got there all okay.

I can tell you that nice warm sunshine over there did me the world of good.

Pauline of course wouldn't rest until she had got the villa spick and span; she said she needed to get it right for when my daughters and their families came out for their holiday. My Daughter Natalie, her Husband Michael, and my Granddaughter Orla, were going out at the end of July.

My other Daughter Michala, her Husband David, and my other two Grandchildren, Maddie, and Joe, were going out early August.

The first week went fine no problems at all; everyday I was feeling a lot better, and a lot stronger.

The second week was a different matter. The second week had just started, and I noticed that the bottle on my Megostomy was filling up a lot quicker than usual; I noticed this later in the day so I left it overnight. This is when most of the feed is pumped into my large bowel, to my surprise the bottle had to be emptied about three times overnight. So in the morning I said to Pauline we had better investigate, the only thing I could think of was that the pipe that went down my jejunostomy into my large bowel was blocked, and it needed flushing out with a syringe.

So I needed a syringe, Pauline looked in the cupboard which had all my medical stuff in it but to no avail no syringe's, it's sod's law when you need something it's never there. Before my last operation I needed to use two a day, and I thought I must have had one left somewhere, so Pauline had to drive to the nearest chemists to get a syringe.

A little while later Pauline arrived back with a couple of syringes, but unfortunately that didn't work, so the next thing to do was to remove the bag, and watch what happened when some more water was pumped down the pipe. To our amazement we saw the pipe had split, so that everything that was supposed to go into my bowel was going into my bottle that meant that I wasn't getting any nutrition. This was when panic set in! A new pipe had to be fitted; I had a new pipe and all the suitable equipment for replacing it, just in case of such an emergency but never thought we would have to do it.

The other little problem we had was, that it been three years previous that Pauline had been shown how to fit a new pipe, and that was quite different, at that time the pipe went down a fistula into my large bowel, and not through my jejunostomy.

I will try to explain this important bit of equipment to you.

If you know what a catheter is like, it is very similar. It is a quite long piece of clear plastic pipe, and at the end that goes into the bowel there is an inflatable bulb, this is to stop it coming out. At the other end it has a plastic washer attached about the size of a fifty pence piece, just after the washer is a valve which was used to inflate the bulb, and then at the end of the pipe, was a threaded connector, this connected to the giving set when I needed the feed.

Well the method of removing the old pipe is to fit a small syringe into the valve, and deflate the bulb, and then it just slides out.

The method of replacing is to put some gel down the hole in the bowel, a little gel on the end of the pipe, slide the pipe into the bowel, then inflate the bulb job done, sounds simple doesn't it. But when it's been so long since you have been shown how to do it, and then on a different part of the body, and you are not too sure what you are doing, it's a bit daunting. So a quick phone call to Hope Hospital, a junior doctor ran through the procedure with me, so between us we managed to get the job done, Pauline said it turned her stomach a bit but anyway the crisis was now over, and it meant we could carry enjoying the Greek sunshine with no more problems.

So from two weeks in the sun, back home to bad weather.

My next Hospital visit was on Tuesday the 11th of August, this was just a HPN clinic visit to check my bloods, my weight, my nutrition, etc. The other thing was to see the doctor, he seemed very pleased with my progress, and my general health. Whilst we were at Hope we got another spare pipe kit, (just in case) as another trip to Kefalonia had been organized for the end of August.

Back home, and on the Wednesday morning I received a phone call from Hope to inform me my magnesium was very low. The doctor said that I looked so well, and that instead of having to go for another infusion I had to up my intake of magnesium powder, from 3 packets a day to 10 a day or even maybe 12, and after a week have a blood test at my local doctors here in Morecambe.

So a week later I had a blood test done, I was getting a bit worried as it was getting close to my flight date. Two days later and I received a phone call from a doctor from Morecambe health centre; he was concerned about the low level of my magnesium. I asked him what the count was, he told me it was 4.8 I said that was good, last week it was 2.4 so it had doubled. I said I knew it should be 7.6 but I would ring Hope and have a word with the doctor and tell them. He said that he would ring also to see if I needed an infusion. When I got hold of a doctor at Hope she told me to keep taking the larger dose, and if I felt unwell whilst I was abroad, have a blood test out there, and if the outcome was bad, to get in contact with her and she would sort something out.

Having this Megostomy connected to my body all of the time caused some problems. The tube was connected to the bottom of a stoma bag by a plastic connecter; the connector was threaded at each end, and a plastic nut which screwed on trapped the tube between them, it was a bit of a crude contraption for such an important job. It also leaked quite a lot, so it had to be wrapped with cloth and covered with a plastic bag; to be honest it was a bit of a pain.

The stoma bag covered my jejunostomy (which in my case was what they called a double barrel); this meant it had two holes. As far as I could understand, my bowel at that point wasn't joined together, so that is probably why there were two holes. Into the bottom hole went the thin pipe, which the food was pumped into my large bowel, (this was the one we had the trouble with before). The pipe had to go through the outer case of the stoma bag, this was fixed by a plastic cone that fit inside the bag, and a rubber diaphragm went over the pipe and over the cone which then clipped together. Out of the top hole, came all the stuff that should have carried on round the bowel, which gives you the nutrition needed to keep you living. This stuff went into my stoma bag, and out through my Megostomy tube which was about 30 inches long, which then again was connected with a crude plastic connecter to this 2.5 litre bottle. The stuff that went down this tube didn't look very nice; basically it was food that had come straight out of the stomach mixed with that green bile, so I had a black cover made to go over the tube, and I used to keep the bottle in a man bag.

The only trouble with this was, the jejunostomy tube came out of my right hand side below my waist, so this caused a problem with my trousers. I thought about getting a kilt, but not being Scottish I dismissed this idea, so I made a hole near the pocket in my trousers to feed the tube through.

I managed okay with it, but I got some funny looks sometimes at a tube coming out of my trousers and into a man bag.

Well time to go back to Kefalonia again, no problems this time, just had time to unwind, and convalesce. Whilst we were there a few different friends came to stay, which was a nice change, we came back home at the beginning of October.

At my last visit to hospital I had been told my last operation would probably be before Christmas.

I had an appointment to see Professor Carlson on the 5th of November, which I duly attended.

I thought when I saw him he would say, I am going to send you for a pre-op, and get you sorted out, no such luck! He said he wanted me to have a contrast study done on my large bowel to make sure it hadn't narrowed. So home we go, and start the waiting game again.

Eventually I received an appointment to go for a contrast study on the 15th of December.

That closed the door on my hopes for the operation happening before Christmas.

15th of December I went and had this contrast study done, it's quite a simple procedure.

Before I went into the ex-ray room I had changed into a operation gown leaving my underpants on. There were two nurses that day, one I knew and a trainee, the nurse I knew went out of the room and left me with the trainee, she said to me just go into that side room and remove your underpants, I asked why because I didn't usually have to remove them, she said something might need to be injected up your bottom, I remarked you will be lucky get much up there and told her why. When the nurse I knew came back I told her about the trainee wanting me to take my underpants off, the trainee went bright red and the nurse said she was hoping for an early Christmas present.

The procedure was that a dye is injected down my feeding pipe into my large bowel, and an ex-ray is taken whilst it is going down to see if there are any restrictions.

I knew the doctor that was doing the procedure due to my many visits to this department, he told me there would have to be a meeting after the x-ray had been studied, but it looked okay to him.

So a few days later good news, there were no restrictions in my bowel, and the operation could go ahead. I received an appointment for my pre-op for the 15th January, also a letter telling me I was on the Professors operating list, which could be up to 10 weeks.

Christmas and the New Year came and went, and by the way, I am getting quite attached to my man bag now, I am hoping that I don't want to keep it after I have got rid of my bottle.

So the 15th of January and off down the motorway to Hope for my pre-op, it all went smoothly. Back home and on the Friday following the pre-op nurse rang to inform me I had a water infection, she said she was informing my GP, so I had to go and collect some antibiotics from the doctors at Morecambe and a week later I had to take a sample back to them for testing.

On the Monday a letter came from Hope, informing me that I had been taken off the operating list until my water infection had been cleared up. Two weeks later I got the all clear; and there's me getting paranoid again, thinking its going to be the middle of the year before I get my operation.

My next trip to Hope was on the 8th of February to the HNP clinic for my 6 month check up; as it happened we bumped into Professor Carlson in the shop in the hospital plaza. He asked how I was, I told him that I felt very well and my water infection was all sorted out. He told me that I was quite near the top of the list now and said it would be about 6 weeks to my operation. Which I thought was strange as I had received a letter telling me I had been taken off the list. If Professor Carlson was right I thought the end of March or the beginning of April for the operation that's not so bad.

Back home again, there was no news from the HPN clinic which was good news, which meant that all my bloods were okay, and my nutrition was okay. On Friday the 16th of February, Allison the Professors sectary rang to tell me that they had had a cancellation for an operation next Friday the 26th of February, and would I be available to take it. I said yes, I couldn't believe my luck. I bet you cant guess the next bit, about 10 minutes later Allison rang back to tell me I couldn't have the operation, as they had not received conformation about my water infection being cleared up from the doctors at Morecambe. So Pauline got on the case, she rang the doctors in Morecambe and told them in no uncertain terms what she thought about there system. With a bit of ringing back and forth it all got sorted out, about 1 hour later and Allison rang back to tell me everything was on track again, and she would send a letter early next week.

CHAPTER NINETEEN

Hopefully the last operation

I arrived at Hope on ward B2 about 11.45 on the Thursday morning the 25th of February as the Professor wanted to see me before his afternoon clinic.

The operation was to be the reversal of the double barrel, or in other words to close the loop jejunostomy, which involved cutting open the area around the jejunostomy, removing some of the bowel from each side, join the bowel back together, put back under the skin and stitch it up. I had been told it was a straightforward procedure, and should take from 3/4 to 1-1/2 hours.

Professor Carlson came to see me in the visitor's room about 1pm, and told me I had to have my blood taken and tested to see if I was okay for the operation. He said he would be back after his clinic, and hopefully the results of the blood test would be back, he said if there was anything wrong it could be sorted out overnight.

I got settled in my bed on the ward about 1-30, then shortly after one of his junior doctors called Mark came to take my blood. He said he needed to put a canula in my arm. Now from previous experiences I know that doctors aren't very good at this, especially junior doctors. Anyway Mark started this assault on my arm, it took 5 attempts and he still didn't manage to get canula in my arm, my arms looked like a dart board. So he decided to just take some blood (which by the way he managed) and come back later to try to fit a canula. A little later on a nurse called Cassy I knew from the last time I was on this ward came to fill in all the relevant forms, and do all the other tests they need to do. Just before the Professor was about to arrive Mark appeared with a tray saying I have got to get a canula into you, I thought oh no not another ten minutes of sheer pain, my arms were turning black and blue from his last attempts, anyway to my surprise he got it straight into a vein first time.

As promised the Professor arrived at about 6pm, and told me my potassium level was high and my magnesium level was low, and I would have to have an infusion over 12 hours to build my magnesium up. Then I signed the consent form after he had gone through all the pros and cons about the operation and the bits that could go wrong.

So if my bloods were okay in the morning my operation would take place early Friday morning.

On the Friday morning about 6am a nurse arrived and took some blood, so when the Professor arrived he had the results, and everything was okay. It was all systems go and he would see me soon in the operating theatre. The porter came for me about 10am, and with a bit of waiting around in the operation waiting area I was eventually wheeled into the anaesthetic room about 10-30.

I had been told the operation should only take between $\frac{3}{4}$ to 1-1/2 hours at most, so you can imagine I was confused when I came round in the recovery room at about 3-15pm.

I was wheeled back to the ward at approximately 3-45.

It was about 5pm when the Professor came to see me, he told me that he had had a right struggle with the operation, and that it had taken the best part of 4hours.

He said it was because the bowel he had separated in my last operation had attached itself to the flap that had been used to fill my abdomen, so he had to cut it away 1mm at a time not do any damage, but when he had finished he said he was very pleased how the connection had gone.

Light heartedly he said he wasn't on duty this weekend, so he said he could have some wine this evening and sleep well knowing the operation had gone well. He also told me that he would see me on Monday morning and if everything went well I could probably go home on Tuesday or Wednesday. My instructions were to eat only very soft food, and only a little at once, hopefully the stoma should start to work early next day. He said not to be concerned if when I went to the toilet for a wee it was a funny colour, because he had injected some dye into my bladder for some reason.

After the Professor had gone I had a bowl of soup, which didn't stop down very long, apparently this is not unusual after having anaesthetic.

So after a good night's sleep, (which is quite unusual in these places), to my surprise my stoma bag had something in it, which pleased me no end.

Saturday was a just a quiet day on the ward, the other fellows on the ward seemed quiet pleasant, not very talkative, but I suppose they all had there own concerns.

The chap in the next bed was a nice elderly gentleman, and eventually we got chatting quite a lot. The funny thing about conversation in hospital is mainly about each others problems, and about treatment and impending operations.

I must tell you about the guy that came on to the ward on the Saturday. He came in about midday, the first thing he did was to get his laptop out to check his e-mails. You can imagine the reaction on the ward, and then he started telling everybody how many times he had been in hospital, and in particular on this ward, so consequently every nurse that came on the ward was interrogated by him. Funny thing but not one of them could remember him.

It really wound him up as all these different nurses came on the ward to see me, every time they came the curtains went round, they wanted to look at how well my leg and tummy had healed. I think most of the guys on the ward were jealous, after the nurse had gone they would remark, how come you are getting all the attention, or what have you got that we haven't, it was all light hearted banter.

Back to the plot, so I continued with my soft food diet, all was going well now my stoma was working well, and I had very little pain from the wound, I wasn't used to this I thought something must go wrong in a bit.

Pauline came to visit Saturday afternoon and evening, which shortened the day enormously.

Sunday morning and I felt great, so I got up and had a shower. A little later Angelo a male nurse I knew quite well came to change the dressing on my wound, it was very dry and there was no infection, it was stapled together and it looked good.

Sunday passed without any hiccups, I had my fair share of visitors. The chap with laptop turned out to be not as much of a prat as I first thought; in fact he lent me his laptop to watch a film, *Pearl Harbour* if my memory serves me right.

I had a bad nights sleep on the Sunday night, but Monday morning remarkably I didn't feel too bad.

It was about 8.30am when the Professor arrived, he asked me how I was feeling, and he was very pleased that everything was working, and that my blood pressure and temperature was okay.

I asked the Professor about the operation and how come I was allowed to eat so soon after my operation, and proceeded to tell him about having to wait a couple of days before I could have anything at eat at Lancaster after my operation there. He said that the bowl healed very quickly, and if he was to go back into the area that he had operated on a few days later, he would be hard pressed to find the part of the bowel that he had joined. He also remarked that he couldn't understand why I wasn't allowed to eat sooner at Lancaster.

With that discussion out of the way he said when would you like to go home? With delight in my face I said as soon as possible.

He said I could go home this afternoon, he would have to get my blood tested, and if everything was okay I could go home and everything would be arranged by my GP and district nurse back home. Mark the junior doctor was with the professor, I showed the professor my arm where Mark had tried to put the canula, it looked a right mess it was all bruised. He said to him did you do that? He said yes, the Professor said to him you Donkey.

This must have been my shortest stay in hospital.

Monday morning was a bit hectic to say the least; first to arrive was the blood nurse, then a sister with a doctor, then the pharmacist, then the stoma nurse, then another doctor I hadn't seen before. He said he had helped the Professor with my operation, he told me how difficult it had been and he didn't want any more like that.

He was very pleased with my condition and wanted to look at my wound, which he was also pleased with.

So by 2-30pm I was armed with loads of literature, diet plans, and tablets.

My next trip to Hope, all being well would be in six weeks to see the Professor.

CHAPTER TWENTY

Home for good

So 4 years and 2 months later and I am back in one piece, no more distal feed, very limited medication, just to keep an eye on my weight and hope I have enough bowel left to give me enough nutrients to keep me up to scratch.

I would still have to go to HPN clinic every six months for a while for all the checks.

So fingers crossed all will be okay.

I had been home about a week and a rash appeared on my forehead and above my right eye. Slightly concerned about this I made an appointment with my GP. When I went to see him he told me I had shingles, and with it being over my eye I had to go back to see him if it got worse as it could take my sight in that eye. He gave me some antibiotics and I asked what caused it, he said it could be trauma from the operation. I thought that's all I need to loose my sight now after all I had been through.

Good news, it all cleared up after a couple of weeks.

Now I was back in one piece I was still left with a colostomy or a stoma bag, I had to learn to live with this for the rest of my life; there was no way this could be reversed. This didn't come without its problems, now my bowel was working properly I had to learn how to look after my colostomy and my stoma bag, and when to empty it. You have no control over this part of your body so the bag used to fill at the most inconvenient times. The other problem was the stoma bag would come off sometimes, this of course usually happened at night time when I was in bed, so you can imagine the mess we had to sort out in the middle of the night. I thought that after my last operation I would have done with all the mess, but apparently not. After a week or so I went to see our local stoma nurse, she told me that a lot of people that have to wear a stoma bag have a lot of problems keeping them on their body, apparently the body sometimes secretes a oily substance which stops the bag from sticking.

Before I left hospital Professor Carlson had advised me to wear a wide body belt; this was to give support to my abdomen and also to help prevent hernias. Our local stoma nurse got this sorted out, it took a few attempts to get the right belt, I couldn't believe the amount of different belts available.

Not long after I had been home I received an appointment to go and see the Professor on February the 26th.

He seemed very pleased with my condition, and how the wound had healed. I told him Pauline and I were going to our Villa in May. He said it might be a good idea to have my bloods done at Morecambe before I went away, so if I had any problems it could be sorted. He said he would like to see me at the end of July or early August, I told him my next appointment at HPN clinic was early August and he told me to make an appointment to see him around that time.

As recommended I had my bloods checked mid April all the results came normal, I couldn't believe that things were going right for a change.

We went out to our Villa mid May until mid July; it was nice to go out there without loads of medical equipment for a change.

Back home and I was feeling as good as I had in a long time, my weight had increased and I felt a great deal stronger too. My appointment to see Professor Carlson was on the 29th of July, and my appointment for HPN clinic was on the 3rd of August.

At my appointment with the Professor he commented on how well I looked, and then he wanted to look at all my body where my operations had been, he checked my entire abdomen for any hernias. He also wanted to know how my digestion was, and a description of the waste that was going into my stoma bag. He also wanted to know if I was managing with my stoma bag and if I was keeping it on my body any better. The next thing he wanted was for me to go and have some full body photographs done, he said he could arrange it for the next time I was down at Hope, I told him that was next Tuesday for HPN clinic, he said that wouldn't be a problem.

Now I thought with the Professor thinking I looked so well, and everything being okay, he would say I don't need to see you again, (how wrong can you be).

He told me he wanted to see me in six months time, and before he saw me he wanted me to have a colonoscopy, and as it would be five years since my original cancer scare he wanted me to have a CT scan as well. I suppose it was something for me to look forward to.

Back home and on the Monday morning the post arrived with my appointment with the Photographer for Tuesday morning before my HPN clinic appointment.

My appointment at HPN was for 2pm so everything worked well. After doing my top model bit we went to Scots bistro for lunch then I duly attended my appointment at the HPN clinic.

They were all very pleased with how well I looked. Kirsten did all her usual tests, and asked all the usual questions, she also commented on how much weight I had put on and said everything must be working.

The next bit was to see the doctor, he was well pleased with me and said to make an appointment for six months and if everything was as good as it was today, the next time I came they would probably discharge me.

Life went on as normal for the rest of 2010; it was late November when I received my next appointment which was for the colonoscopy, on the 4th of January 2011; as before the normal clear out fluid came with instructions, this wasn't as bad as it was before, first I knew the effects, and second it was all going into my stoma bag this time, I just had to empty it on a regular basis so it didn't push the bag off.

At the procedure this time, the camera couldn't go up my bottom, so it was fed through my colostomy which didn't feel half as bad as it did before. I watched the camera go all the way through my bowel, and I must say I was ever so pleased to see that it was all perfect.

The next trip to Hope was on the 25th of January for my HPN clinic appointment, as promised at my last visit I was discharged as everything was good.

My next appointment was to see Professor Carlson on the 27th of January, as per usual a follow up letter was sent to my GP, and I will copy this for you.

DATE/TIME of Appt   27 JANUARY 2011 at 14:30
Clinic: COLORECTAL CLINIC
Type of Appt: Follow-up

I have reviewed Paul today in clinic. He remains very well indeed following the complex intestinal failure and abdominal wall reconstruction jointly by my plastic surgical colleague, Mr. Stuart Watson, and myself, back in March 2009. His abdominal wall remains soundly healed. His appetite is good and he is well himself.

He is shortly going on a cruise of the Far East before returning briefly to this country, then taking off to Kefalonia for the summer.

His quality of life is therefore obviously extremely good, and he has been discharged from follow up by our Home Parenteral Nutrition Clinic. I have reassured Mr. Pringle strongly that all is well, but I have, given the fact that it is almost five years since his original large bowel cancer resection, the complications of which led to his open abdomen and multiple small bowel fistulas, arranged a CT scan of the chest, abdomen and pelvis for him. We have arranged to do this in March, when he is back in the country.

I will write with the results and have arranged to review him in six months.

    The professor omitted to put in this letter the results of my Colonoscopy, which he told me, was clear.

    So just a CT scan to look forward to and fingers crossed everything will be okay.

    The appointment came for the 7th of April, for the scan.

Which I duly attended and I am pleased to say when I received the results everything was clear. So my next trip down to Hope would be to see Professor Carlson later in the year.

We had a lovely trouble-free few months in Kefalonia; I was still having a few problems and the occasional mess with my stoma bag, the hot weather didn't help it seemed to melt the adhesive. But it was a small price to pay after all I had been through, I was lucky to be still alive.

Late August and Michala rang to tell me an appointment had come for me to see the Professor in early September. Our air tickets back home wasn't until early October. Problem solved, Michala managed to rearrange my appointment for the 10th of November.

Back home and before I went down to Hope to see the Professor, I would get my bloods done in Morecambe and take the results down for him to see.

When I went to see him I thought he must give me my marching orders this time - to no avail. He commented on how well I looked. Then he told me what I already knew, that my CT scan was all clear, he then did his usual checks for any development of hernias, and asked all the usual questions.

He then asked if I would give my consent to all the photographs of my body that had been taken throughout my time in hospital, to be used in a medical publication in the British Journal of Surgery. I gave my consent; he then said he would get Allison to send me a consent form for me to sign.

There was no way he was going to let go of me, he said he would like to see me again in 12 months, and if I could have my bloods done before I come that would save me having them done here.

I think the reason he wanted to keep me on his books was I was the third person to have this pioneering operation, and I came through it very well, plus all the photos they took to use for seminars.

So it seems like I will have to go and see him every year, still it's good that he his willing to keep his eye on me.

In conclusion I can't thank Professor Carlson enough for all the care and attention he has given to me throughout my hospital stay and aftercare.

CHAPTER TWENTY ONE

Photographs & Illustrations

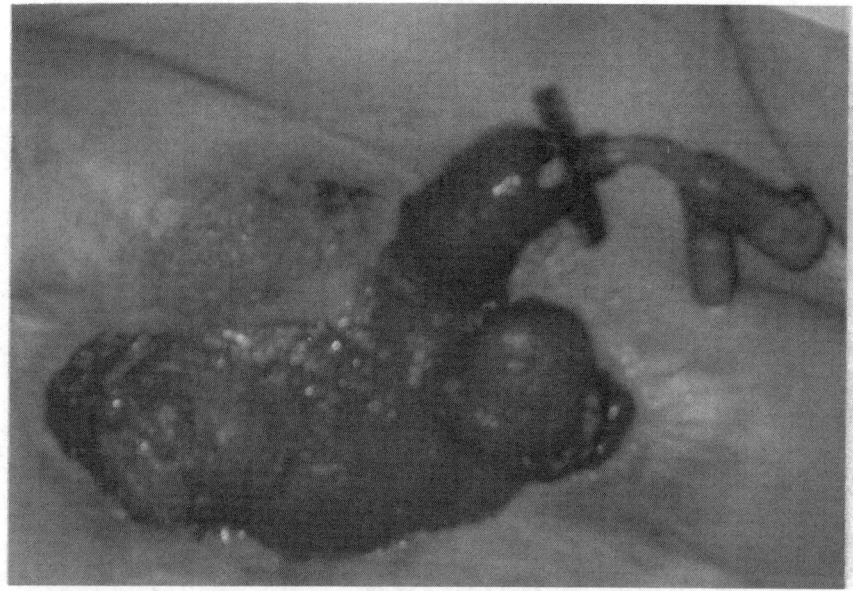

Fistulas with feeding tube going down into bowel.

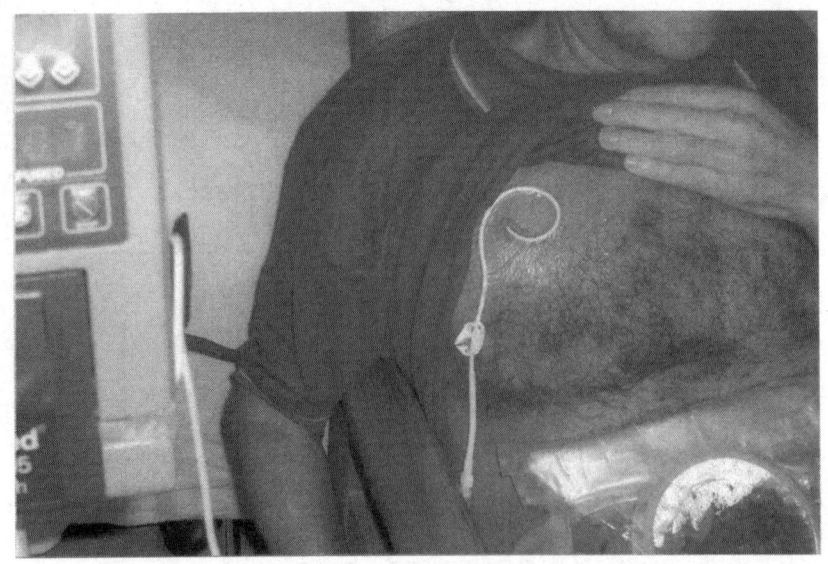

Feeding tube for PTFE going into main artery.

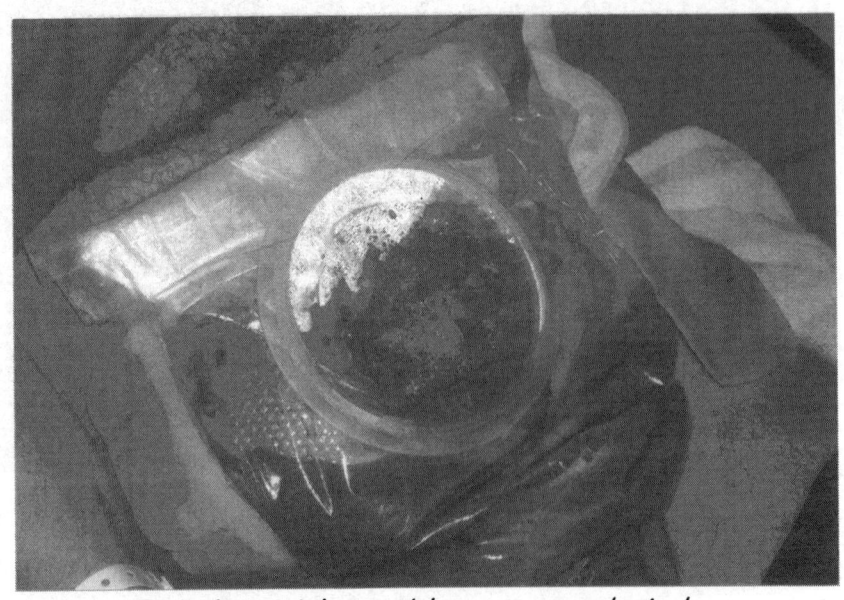

First bag with troublesome round window
that kept leaking.

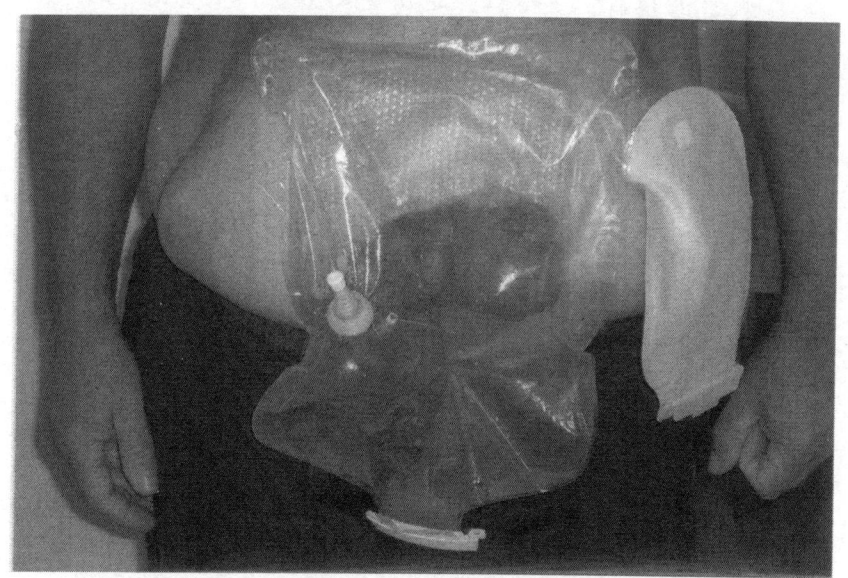

Second bag, with feeding tube going through,
for perative feed. Also stoma bag on my left side.

Me in Kefalonia with feeding tube connected,
pump and bottle on the floor.

My wound care plan sent from hospital for district nurse's attention.

With this plan also came many instructions and charts to fill in.

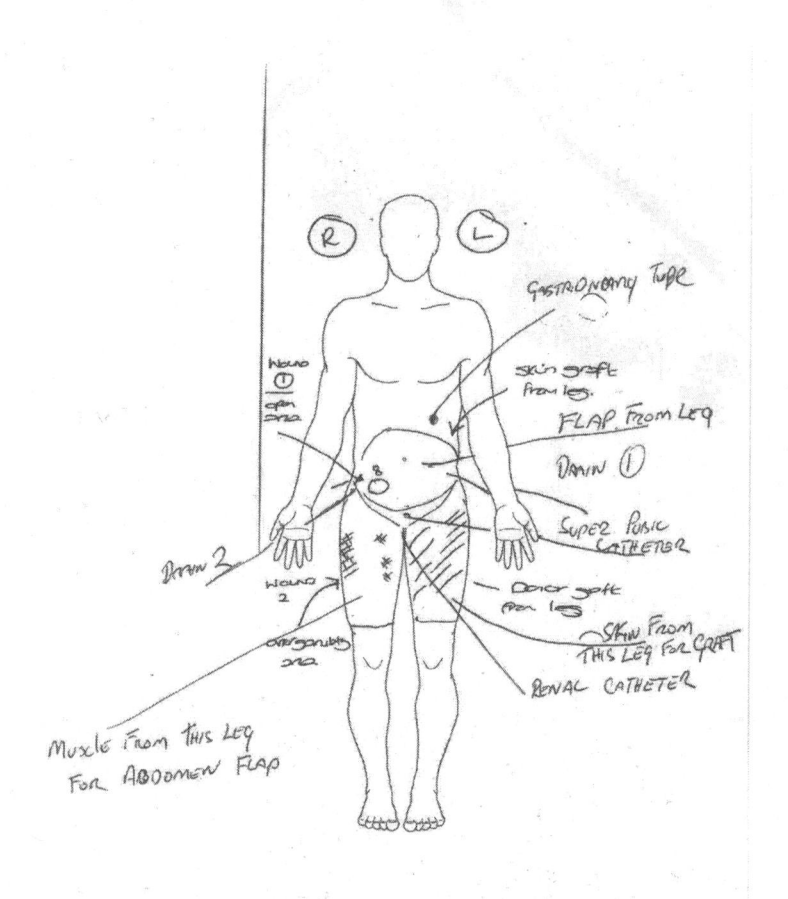

Diagram above used after large operation, to show all wounds and various tubes and drains.